PORTRAITS OF A RADICAL DISCIPLE

RECOLLECTIONS OF JOHN STOTT'S LIFE AND MINISTRY

EDITED BY

CHRISTOPHER J. H. WRIGHT

FOREWORD BY DAVID NEFF

IVP Books

An imprint of InterVarsity Press
Downers Grove, Illinois

InterVarsity Press
P.O. Box 1400, Downers Grove, IL 60515-1426
Internet: www.ivpress.com
E-mail: email@ivpress.com

InterVarsity Press® is the book-publishing division of InterVarsity Christian Fellowship/USA®, a movement of students and faculty active on campus at hundreds of universities, colleges and schools of nursing in the United States of America, and a member movement of the International Fellowship of Evangelical Students. For information about local and regional activities, write Public Relations Dept., InterVarsity Christian Fellowship/USA, 6400 Schroeder Rd., P.O. Box 7895, Madison, WI 53707-7895, or visit the IVCF website at <www.intervarsity.org>.

ISBN 978-0-8308-3810-3

Design: Cindy Kiple
Images: wallpaper pattern: © Bill Noll/iStockphoto
    antique golden frames: © Katrin Solansky/iStockphoto
    images of John Stott: Langham Partnership International

Printed in the United States of America ∞

Library of Congress Cataloging-in-Publication Data

Portraits of a radical disciple: recollections of John Stott's life
and ministry/edited by Christopher J. H. Wright.
    p. cm.
    Includes bibliographical references.
    ISBN 978-0-8308-3810-3 (pbk.: alk. paper)
    1. Stott, John R. W. 2. Church of England—Clergy—Biography. 3.
Anglican Communion—England—Biography. 4
Evangelicalism—Church of England—Biography. I. Wright, Christopher
J. H., 1947-
    BX5199.S8344P67 2011
    283.092—dc23
    [B]

2011023119

P	18	19	16	15	14	13	12	11	10	9	8	7	6	5	4	3	2	1
Y	26	25	24	23	22	21	20	19	18	17	16	15	14	13	12	11		

To Frances Whitehead,
without whom this portrait
would have been very different

CONTENTS

FOREWORD

In this collection of essays remembering John Stott, friends and colleagues call to mind his kindness, his thoughtfulness, his humor and his peculiarities. One of John Stott's unusual abilities was to remember others and call them by name. Many have been surprised that this widely traveled English pastor, whose parish was awash in visitors, remembered them. He could recall the names and faces of people he had only briefly encountered.

I too was amazed at our second encounter that John Stott recognized and remembered me. Years had passed between our meetings and as far as I knew there was nothing that should have made me stand out in his memory.

On that second meeting I divulged one important personal datum: that my parents lived in the birding mecca of the American Southwest. Over 250 species of birds have been documented in Madera Canyon, the northernmost point in the migration of the Elegant Trogon from Central America. When I identified my family home, he announced that he had been there three times. I was impressed.

Like most of those who will read this book, my association with John Stott has been mainly at a distance. But memories of this great preacher are indelibly impressed.

I remember watching him at All Souls, kneeling and earnestly praying before he preached. It was a lesson I took to heart during my own preaching years.

I remember hearing him confess—in order to make a homiletical point with wit and charm—a certain sartorial lust for the bright red necktie of a worshiper seated in the front rows. I remember corresponding with him when I came to *Christianity Today* in the mid-1980s and learning even then of the care with which he focused his writing energies. He had his chosen writing focus (at that time, he was at the halfway point in The Bible Speaks Today), and therefore declined to write original material for *CT*, but he generously offered us the opportunity to adapt anything he had written for our use.

I remember learning theological lessons from him: to integrate social ministry and a Christian concern for current issues with a cross-centered gospel, to sanctify my daily work to the Lord rather than to my career, to see the church as an organism and not a hierarchy, to test evangelical truth in the confidence that it will stand up to close examination.

John R. W. Stott's friends and colleagues will remember him for the many ways he touched their lives. But so will those of us who deeply felt his influence at a distance. May his memory live long.

David Neff

PREFACE

It is often said that the Acts of the Apostles would be better titled "Some Acts of Some Apostles," since most of the apostles of our Lord Jesus Christ are not even mentioned in Acts, and of those who are mentioned, doubtless many more stories could be told. The same could be said of this book: *Portraits of a Radical Disciple: Recollections of John Stott's Life and Ministry*. This is a mere sketch of a man who overflows all attempts to describe him, offered by a tiny few of his many, many friends.

For one of the outstanding gifts that God gave to John Stott, observed by almost every contributor to this collection, was an incredible capacity for friendship. Never did the word *single* seem less appropriate than for this lifelong bachelor. If all the stories were to be recorded of all the friends with something to tell of their encounters with John, we should have an encyclopedia from every corner of the globe.

The limits of a single book imposed a painful selectivity, therefore, and I hasten to offer an apology to any who may feel they too could have laid claim to inclusion among the contributors. There are, of course, many more friends who could indeed have added their brushstrokes to the portrait and enriched the book. But it was impossible to ask everybody even on the long list that was initially compiled when the idea was first conceived. The idea was first envisioned, in fact, by John Stott himself. It was in 2005, during a week while he was in residence at The Hookses (his writing cottage in Wales, much referred to in the following pages), along with Frances Whitehead, Matthew Smith, his study assistant, and myself. I am sure that the idea came to him from a book of the same sort written to commemorate the life and ministry of E. J. H. Nash, popularly known as "Bash." It was Bash who led John Stott to faith in Christ as a schoolboy, and John was one of the contributors to that portrait.[1] John was enormously grateful for the two-volume authorized biography by Timothy Dudley-Smith (as he later was for the more popular-level biography by Roger Steer; both were published by IVP). But he felt that a more personal picture could be painted by those who had known him more intimately over the years—and he insisted it should be a frank and honest portrait, "warts and all," as he put it. He came up with an initial list of people who, he thought, would have some interesting perspectives on different phases of his life and ministry. He asked me if I might be willing to take on the task of inviting them to contribute and then assume full responsibility for the selection and editing of whatever emerged. He insisted that he did not wish to read any of the contributions himself, in order that people should feel free to speak the truth as they saw it without embarrassment. He also intended that the book should be published posthumously, but he later agreed to the request of IVP, who happily accepted the proposal provided it could be published alternatively for his ninetieth birthday, if he should reach that great milestone.

As contributions came in over the following years, it was hard to know how to organize such a collection. It felt like a living art gallery that could be arranged along various possible thematic lines. The structure finally chosen is approximately chronological, though of course some of the contributors are people whose friendship with John has spanned many decades. I am very grateful to Eleanor Trotter at IVP, who worked with me editorially throughout this project and came up with many suggestions and proposals that have enhanced the book immeasurably.

It only remains for me to thank all those who sent me their recollections of John, both long and short. It has been a privilege to see our mutual friend through so many different pairs of eyes, and to share in the overwhelming gratitude we all feel to God for the gift of having known and loved this gentle giant, and to have been the objects of his gracious and generous affection.

Somehow it seems very fitting that I am writing this preface in the little room on the ground floor of 12 Weymouth Street, which has been Frances Whitehead's office for all the years she has worked for John Stott, with my back to the tiny apartment in Bridford Mews where John met innumerable friends over the years. What volumes of work have passed up and down the stairs between here and there! What quantities of manuscripts, files, sermons, lectures and correspondence were meticulously organized here by Frances! How many corners of the earth have received letters from John, typed here by Frances! How many visitors put their heads round this door to be greeted by Frances, on their way to a meeting with John! And how good of her to allow me the use of her office, while she is taking a short holiday, to complete the final editing of this portrait.

Frances, herself now in her mid-eighties (at the time I write), is still pleased to be known as "John Stott's Secretary," and has worked tirelessly for him for more than fifty years. There is no doubt whatsoever that, under God, no other human being has contributed more to the worldwide fruitfulness of the ministry of John Stott. Her ministry and gifts were indispensable to the fullest exercise of his. Without her, this portrait would have been very different. So with boundless affection, gratitude and respect, I dedicate to her this portrait of the man whose life and ministry she so selflessly enhanced and enabled.

Chris Wright
September 2010

ABBREVIATIONS

AGE	Accountability/Advisory Group of Elders
ALCOE	Asian Leadership Conference on Evangelism
ASO	All Souls Orchestra
BST	The Bible Speaks Today
CICCU	Cambridge Inter-Collegiate Christian Union
CLADE	Congress Latinoamericano de Evangelizacion (Latin American Congress on Evangelism)
CMS	Church Mission Society
EFAC	Evangelical Fellowship in the Anglican Communion
ELT	Evangelical Literature Trust
ESV	English Standard Version
FEET	Fellowship of European Evangelical Theologians
IFES	International Fellowship of Evangelical Students
IVCF	InterVarsity Christian Fellowship/Inter-Varsity Christian Fellowship
IVF	Inter-Varsity Fellowship (UK) (now UCCF)
IVP	Inter-Varsity Press (U.K.) or InterVarsity Press (U.S.)
KJV	King James Version
LICC	London Institute for Contemporary Christianity
MWE	Movement for World Evangelisation
NEAC	National Evangelical Anglican Conference
NECSE	National Evangelical Conference on Social Ethics (1978)
NIV	New International Version

OCR   Old Combination Room (of Trinity College,
        Cambridge)
SCM   Student Christian Movement
TEDS   Trinity Evangelical Divinity School
UCCF   Universities and Colleges Christian Fellowship
WCC   World Council of Churches

John Stott: A Timeline

April 27, 1921	Born in London
September 1929	Oakley Hall School, Gloucestershire
September 1935	Rugby School, Warwickshire
February 13, 1938	Conversion after hearing Eric (Bash) Nash preach
1938-1940	Decides to be ordained; embraces pacifism
October 1940	Enters Trinity College, Cambridge
October 1942	Begins study of theology
June 1943	Graduates with double first
October 1944	Graduate studies in theology at Ridley Hall, Cambridge
December 21, 1945	Ordained deacon in St. Paul's Cathedral Becomes curate at All Souls
November 1946	Lives on the streets disguised as a tramp
September 26, 1950	Instituted as rector of All Souls parish
August 1952	Discovers remote area near a Welsh farmhouse called The Hookses Moves to All Souls Rectory, No. 12 Weymouth Street
1952	Leads university mission at Cambridge
January 1954	First book, *Men with a Message*, published
1954	Buys The Hookses in Pembrokeship Supports Billy Graham in Harringay Crusade

1955	Billy Graham's Wembley Crusade
November 1955	Assistant missioner to Billy Graham at Cambridge
1956	Frances Whitehead appointed secretary
November 1956	Sails from Southampton for missions in U.S.A. and Canada
December 1956	Christmas with Grahams in Montreat, North Carolina
1958	Writes *Basic Christianity* Missions in Australia Sir Arnold Stott dies
June 1959	Appointed chaplain to the Queen
Spring 1962	Second visit to Africa Visits to Keswick Convention begin
December 1964	First of six visits to Urbana Student Missions Convention, University of Illinois
January 1966	Lily Stott dies
October 18, 1966	Public clash with Martyn Lloyd-Jones
April 1967	First National Evangelical Congress at Keele University
1968	Begins editing and contributing to The Bible Speaks Today series
December 1970	Speaks for third time at Urbana Student Missions Convention
April 1971	Begins to divert book royalties to Evangelical Literature Trust
1972	Moves into Bridford Mews flat

Autumn 1972	Guest lecturer at Trinity Evangelical Divinity School, Deerfield, Illinois
January 1974	Scholars program begins which will become Langham Partnership International
July 1974	Keynote address at Lausanne Congress Pleads at Lausanne for new balance between evangelism and social action Writes commentary on Lausanne Covenant he has drafted
1975	Becomes Rector Emeritus of All Souls; Michael Baughen becomes rector
November 1975	Adviser at fifth assembly of World Council of Churches First becomes known as "Uncle John"
June 1976	At Bathurst Inlet dives in search of drowned Jacob Avadlukl
November 26, 1976	Reopening of All Souls with Waldegrave Hall beneath
Summer 1977	Second visit to South America; visits Galapagos Islands
January 1978	Chairs drafting of Willowbank (Bermuda) Friendship with Chris Wright begins
December 19, 1978	Last meeting with Martyn Lloyd-Jones
April to May 1980	In Eastern Europe Mark Labberton succeeds Tom Cooper as study assistant
1981	Visits India and Bangladesh; meets Mother Teresa

January 1982	London Institute of Contemporary Christianity launched
April 4, 1982	Bash dies; John conducts memorial service
Summer 1982	Michael Baughen becomes bishop of Chester
January 1983	Joins royal family at Sandringham
	Richard Bewes becomes rector of All Souls
1985	Declines to allow his name to go forward as bishop of Winchester
June 1984	Completes *The Cross of Christ*
July 1989	Lausanne II, Manila, Philippines
August 1989	Sails up Amazon
1992	*The Contemporary Christian* published
July 7, 1993	Debates human sexuality with Bishop John Spong
July 1996	Successfully sights snowy owl at Cambridge Bay, Canada
1996	John Yates succeeds Nelson Gonzales as study assistant
May 1998	Embolisms impair eyesight; gives up driving
January to February 1999	With John Yates to China, Thailand and Hong Kong
1999	*Evangelical Truth* launched at IFES World Assembly

January 31, 2000	With study assistant Corey Widmer in Kenya and Uganda; time with David Zac Niringiye
September 2001	Appoints Chris Wright as his successor as international director of Langham Partnership International
February 2002	With Corey Widmer in East Asia
New Year 2003	Completes *Why I Am a Christian*
April 10, 2005	Listed by *Time* magazine as one of 100 most influential people in the world
August 20, 2006	Falls and breaks hip
2007	*The Living Church* published
June 8, 2007	Moves to College of St. Barnabas, Lingfield, Surrey
July 17, 2007	Preaches at Keswick forty-five years after first visit
July 27, 2011	Dies at the age of ninety

EARLY AND
FORMATIVE YEARS

THE LOVING UNCLE

CAROLINE BOWERMAN

Caroline Bowerman is John Stott's niece; her mother was John's sister. She is a recently retired schoolteacher, living in London. John was also her godfather.

Wumby Dumby (the first name I used to give him), and then Uncle Johnnie, has been a very special person to me all my life, not only because he was my uncle and godfather, but also because of his continual loving interest, support and friendship.

As far back as I can remember, Uncle Johnnie was a part of Christmas. Probably feeling utterly exhausted by all the pre-Christmas work and celebrations at All Souls and his travels, he usually arrived on Christmas Eve in time to listen with us to the Nine Lessons and Carols service from King's College, Cambridge. He appeared to be able promptly to put aside his working life and give this time to the family, including three very demanding nieces. He always loved Christmas dinner and especially the brandy butter, which he heaped onto his pudding even in his tee-total days!

Uncle Johnnie spoke about his travels in a way that always captured our attention and often gave us an edited slide show of his most recent overseas visit, although there were always plenty of pictures of birds, so I doubt that they were ever edited very rigorously! He also held us spellbound with stories from his childhood. He told us how his behavior sometimes led him into trouble with his parents. For example, during the sermon at the All Souls morning service, seated in a front pew on the balcony, he and my aunt occupied themselves by screwing up pieces of paper and then surreptitiously dropping them onto the hats of the ladies sitting below.

Throughout my childhood, Uncle Johnnie gave me really good Christian books to read. Often, when he was staying with us or when we were with him at The Hookses, he would read them to me at bedtime. Sometimes he also shared his faith and prayed in a very child-friendly way.

He was always so keen for us to visit his beloved Hookses, and he was sometimes able to be there with us too. Those were very special times. It was there that I first saw how hard he worked. And he was delighted when his great-nephew, John, aged nine, announced that he loved The Hookses so much that he planned to spend his honeymoon there!

When I came to London to train as a teacher, Uncle Johnnie maintained his loving support. He encouraged me to attend All Souls and invited me to some delicious lunches and teas at the rectory, welcoming and including my new friends too. It was only then that I discovered his complete dedication, some of his other gifts in ministry, and his importance and popularity within the church.

Family was always very important to Uncle Johnnie. Even as a child I could see how close he was to his mother and how he really missed her when she died, just as he did his two sisters when they later died. Uncle Johnnie conducted my wedding to Roger and came as quickly as he could to see our children after they were born. He also took a keen interest in his great-nieces and -nephews. On separate occasions he even invited his two great-nieces, Hannah and Emily, to royal Garden Parties.

Another time he invited my sister Sarah and me to go to Buckingham Palace with him and Frances Whitehead when he was receiving his CBE (Commander of the Order of the British Empire) award from the Queen. He always tried to join family gatherings, and after my mother (his last remaining sister) died, he spent each Christmas with us.

For me, Uncle Johnnie has always been the same—a very humble, compassionate, caring, loving and just person, and an extremely hard worker (setting himself targets that most people would find hard to achieve). My aunt often used to tease him that she could hear "the chains clanging as he drove his slaves on"! Throughout my life I have clearly seen his desire to serve Jesus, who was so clearly and completely at the center of his life.

2

THE WEDDING SERMON

MICHAEL GREEN

Michael Green was principal of St. John's College, Nottingham, rector of St. Aldates, Oxford, and professor of evangelism at Regent College, Vancouver. A prolific author and still active in retirement since 1996, he lives near Oxford.

I first came across John Stott at Iwerne Minster, a Christian house party which took place in Dorset three times a year for the purpose of winning and training boys for Christ from the public school system. When I was a teenager there in the 1950s, John would occasionally come down to the camp to speak or just to be with us. He had been a leader at these house parties prior to his ordination, but of course his new responsibilities at All Souls made it more difficult for him to get away. The Rev. E. J. H. Nash, known universally as "Bash," had taken particular care of John Stott, going out of his way to visit him, taking him out to tea (which combined deep conversation with cucumber sandwiches) and writing him letters (by hand) that always included a spiritual thought. As I recall, Bash wanted John to become archbishop of Canterbury!

After that, I did not see a lot of John for a few years. However, my closest friend, Julian Charley, became his curate, first at All Souls and then at the Clubhouse,[1] so I heard what was going on there pretty often and could sense a new vigor and vision moving from John through the Church of England. John was keen to spread his influence beyond London and soon gathered a group of young clergy whom he called Eclectics (following the example of Charles Simeon, who had hosted a group by the same name). It was a privilege to belong to those early Eclectics meetings. We would spend a day together from time to time, sharing fellowship, listening to a major theological paper and enjoying a powerful devotional time.

At the other end of the spectrum, John was at that time writing Christian puzzles at Christmastime for *Crusade* magazine!

From those early encounters I knew him well enough to ask if Rosemary and I might be married in his smaller church, St. Peter's, Vere Street. This was because both of us lived in inaccessible places, and so it made sense to have the wedding in central London. John agreed not only to the location but also to preparing us for marriage and preaching at the wedding, while my father tied the knot. We had just one session with him in marriage preparation, I recall, but it has enabled us to love each another happily for over fifty years!

At the wedding John preached on 1 Thessalonians 5:10: "[He] died for us, that, whether we wake or sleep, we should live together with him" (KJV). John knew that I was a New Testament buff, and I remember him modestly apologizing that he had taken the verse somewhat out of context in order to emphasize the word *together*. We were delighted.

But one aspect of that wedding always sticks in my mind. John invited me to stay the night before the wedding at the rectory. So I slept on the floor of his study. And I was amazed at how early it was in the morning that John came in to study the Bible and to pray. It is a lesson I have never forgotten.

Of course I have seen him many times since—often at conferences when we were both speaking, and more recently in his retirement home where, in restricted circumstances and despite failing health, he remained the gracious, perceptive leader he has always been. But I shall remember him best for that wedding in September 1957.

3

THE COMPULSIVE WORKER,
BUT A RARE SPELLING MISTAKE

JOHN EDDISON

*After a curacy in Tunbridge Wells, John Eddison joined the staff
of Scripture Union in 1942 and retired in 1980. For most of this
time he was a colleague of Bash and helped him at the camps at
Iwerne Minster. He also ran the junior camps for preparatory
schoolboys at Swanage.*

I first met John Stott at Beachborough Park, near Folkestone, in
the summer of 1938. This was where Eric Nash (Bash) held his
house parties before the war drove them into deeper country in
Dorset, where there was also ample scope for farm work in the
neighborhood of Iwerne Minster. I was standing at the time at the
top of a staircase when this fresh-faced, smiling boy of seventeen
came prancing up. He was just back from France and was clutch-
ing a bottle of wine. Clearly he had not yet had the chance to discover that this was not the sort of gift you offered to Bash, a confirmed teetotaler!

For the next eight years I saw a lot of John Stott. While he was
still at Rugby School, I paid one or two visits to Rugby, where in

some local hostelry he would arrange a large tea party for boys whom he wanted to interest in the camps. So successful was he that in 1939, on our last visit there, there were no fewer than fifteen Rugby pupils present.

When he reached Cambridge, John took over the secretarial responsibility for the camps, which, with all the war-time restrictions and regulations, was an enormous task. How he managed it, and collected a first-class honors degree at the same time, has always mystified and amazed me. He turned the camps from a slightly amateur organization into a well-oiled machine, relieving Bash of a huge burden. He was a compulsive worker, and even if there wasn't work to be done, he always found some anyway. I am inclined to think that he could in some ways have spared himself. His successor, Philip Thompson, was able to approach the work in a slightly more relaxed manner, without any apparent loss of efficiency.

In 1942 I joined the staff of Scripture Union as an assistant to Eric Nash, and for the next three years I worked very closely with John and saw a great deal of him. Even then he gave the most memorable talks, and to this day, well over sixty years later, I can remember one particularly vivid illustration. More than once I heard him tell the story of the cross in a most moving way.

When the boys had gone home at the end of a camp, it was customary for the few of us leaders who had remained to tidy up, to relax over supper in a local cottage. That was when we would see the playful, almost mischievous, side of John. I remember too that on one such occasion I found myself "one-up" on John. I told him that the word *withhold* had two "hs"—John was sure it had only one. Somebody produced a Bible, and it was only on the evidence of Genesis 22:12 ("because you have not withheld from me your son") that we were able to convince John that for once he was wrong!

At the end of the summer camp in 1945, John finally relinquished the secretarial work, and I took it over for two years until Philip Thompson was able and free to do so. I drove John home that day, and I got the feeling that for him it was the end of an era; he was closing one chapter of his life and preparing for something new. Iwerne had one or two further visits from him and of course enjoyed his enduring encouragement and support. But it was time for him to move on, and his gifts required greater scope and a wider canvas. I am glad to say we kept in touch. He stayed with us more than once, and we met from time to time. My links with the Iwerne Minster camps continued for many years, and it was not hard to see the incalculable debt that they owed to John.

The Young Defender of the Faith

OLIVER BARCLAY

Oliver Barclay was General Secretary of UCCF from 1964 to 1980. He was cofounder of the journal Science and Christian Belief *and active in the movement* "Christians in Science." *He is now retired and lives in Leicester.*

John Stott arrived at Trinity College, Cambridge, straight from school in 1940, two years after I had arrived there myself. He completed the first part of his degree in French and German in two years and then went on to study theology for his third and fourth years before moving on to Ridley Hall, an Anglican theological college in Cambridge, to complete his training for ordination in the Church of England.

As soon as he arrived in Cambridge, John immediately found fellowship in the college group of the strongly evangelical Cambridge Inter-Collegiate Christian Union (CICCU), and before long he was seen as its obvious informal leader. The Cambridge Christian scene at that time needs describing. Almost every college had a full-time Anglican chaplain, with some weeknight activities and services in the college chapel on Sundays. Without exception these chaplains were not evangelical but held a mixture of high church and liberal theology. The theology faculty was then almost uniformly liberal. These chaplains and professors were very scornful of evangelicals, often criticizing their beliefs or ridiculing them.

That era was a high point of an aggressive, rationalistic liberalism. To study theology was proving a death trap for many who had come to university with a simple faith. In Cambridge the Student Christian Movement (SCM) had become very liberal too, and the CICCU had split from it in 1920. By the time John Stott arrived, the SCM's college groups were in decline and the CICCU provided the only lively evangelical fellowship. It was a battle to maintain orthodox faith.

The CICCU arranged excellent united Saturday night Bible expositions and Sunday night evangelistic services, as well as a smaller daily prayer meeting for core members. Each college group had a weekly Bible study, which usually ended with coffee and discussion late into the evening. The Trinity College CICCU group of about twelve members usually attended the college chapel services on Sundays as a matter of duty, but it was the CICCU that represented a lively Christian witness. To me it was a most convincing fellowship of genuine faith and life. The CICCU group tried to reach and befriend each new generation of Christian freshmen as they arrived. They did this for me, in spite of my initial doctrinal vagaries imbibed from school religious education. I had been converted at school and the CICCU had drawn me in and sorted out my basic doctrinal thinking. But I was not a mature Christian and had a lot to learn.

John Stott, although also a young Christian, had arrived better taught than I had been, thanks to the Iwerne Minster camps and the Rugby School Christian Union, through which he had been converted two years earlier. We were both learning fast and acknowledged that we owed a huge debt to the CICCU. We quickly became good friends, often walking in the college courts and gardens, discussing things, and in later years going out on bicycles birdwatching. However, I had become more interested than he in apologetics, particularly as I was a science student and had to face different questions from those with which he was familiar. We helped each other through the battles, along with others in the college group.

As the Second World War continued and student numbers shrank, Trinity College intended to close its Sunday chapel services. However, John and I, along with other CICCU members in Trinity, asked if we could run them so that they could continue. In our minds this was a means of outreach to the number of fairly nominal Christians who liked to go. The college agreed and John became our key speaker. He also had an exceptionally good singing voice and had previously sung solos in chapel. He often read the Bible lessons and had even won a college prize for the best reader in chapel. He was an example to us all of an extremely disciplined life, always leaving the college Bible studies at 9:30 p.m. to go to bed, even when discussion was in full swing, so he could rise by 6 a.m. for his "quiet time." Then, having skimmed through *The Times*, he would leave early after breakfast to go to the library, where he worked very hard at his studies.

John also had considerable responsibilities in the administration of the Iwerne Minster camps run by Bash, through whom he had been converted. Camp gave an excellent grounding in basic Christian doctrine and living, including the disciplined habit of daily prayer and Bible study. "Bash campers" had been CICCU presidents for several years in succession and were a distinct group of fine leaders in the college groups and in personal evangelism.

They were, however, inclined to be suspicious of wider interests and especially anything that could be deemed to be "intellectual." When I told one of the campers that I was very interested in modern poetry (T. S. Eliot and W. H. Auden), I was told not to advertise this or some would think I was going astray! Bash's view on these things stemmed largely from the devastating effect on many students of studying theology and the sad state of the SCM who pursued such issues. As a result, Bash and many campers could be very critical of anything other than basic Bible study and evangelism. Bash stressed "the simple gospel," and he rightly discerned that most students had not really understood this but held very misleading ideas of the nature of the Christian message. The emphasis on direct evangelism was necessary, but unfortunately it was accompanied by a negative attitude to culture and even to apologetics. Only later, when his campers found that a message ideal for schoolboys was not by itself enough for those who went out into the workplace, did Bash begin to appreciate the need for others to provide teaching on areas of Christian discipleship that he himself could not supply. John, as he moved through his studies, probably helped Bash to see the point of tackling such wider issues. In later years Bash became less negative, while always still stressing the importance of the simple gospel.

John was also involved with the college CICCU group and was a fine personal evangelist. More than one of his student friends professed conversion through his help, and he was soon skillful at helping young and immature believers. When he moved to Ridley Hall, he often led Bible studies in different colleges. I remember a very young Christian falling asleep while John was still speaking and having to be quietly kicked awake to save his embarrassment. So John's speaking style was clearly not yet honed and at its best!

When John began the second half of his degree, studying theology, the battles became fierce. Lecturers took delight in pointing out the difficulties for traditional faith, and he had to study their books too. I do not think others realized how acutely difficult John found this at times, just because he was so honest-minded. I well remember him sitting in my college room virtually in tears, saying that if he could not work his way through the liberal teaching, his ministry would be destroyed and he would be left with no

ability to preach a word from God. Bash could not help him, and
at that time there were no evangelical scholars available to do so
either.

Thankfully, however, one of the former campers, John Wenham, a part-time curate (assistant pastor) in a church in Cambridge, who was also doing postgraduate studies in theology at the
university, was developing into an excellent theological thinker.
He introduced John to the writings of Benjamin Warfield and
other, mainly American, conservative scholars. Wenham had a
habit of lending or giving away key books. He befriended John and
encouraged him to realize that there were others who were tackling these tough theological issues too. John Wenham was involved, with the British Inter-Varsity Fellowship (IVF), in the establishment of Tyndale House, an evangelical research library in
Cambridge specializing in biblical and theological studies at the
highest levels of scholarly rigor. John later acknowledged his debt
to scholars like John Wenham and others at Tyndale House. He
could not quickly find answers to all the problems raised and he
had to put some of them into a mental "pending" file for future attention. However, he accepted with new confidence that if our
Lord and the apostles taught the authority and reliability of the
Bible, then the Bible would prove reliable and authoritative. This
confidence was confirmed when he constantly saw the spiritual
power of the word of God as it was preached. While at Ridley, John
had the opportunity to visit neighboring villages to preach in small
churches. These were his first efforts to preach to less academic
congregations, which began to broaden his scope in new ways.

I do not think that John Stott's time in Cambridge did a lot to
lay foundations for writing later books like *Issues Facing Christians Today* or his passion for emphasizing the place of social
action in relation to evangelism within a holistic understanding
of Christian mission and ministry. He was too busy with the immediate need to work out his own theological position and to

take the opportunities of personal witness that the student world offers. However, he had certainly learned that you have to "contend for the faith that was once for all entrusted to the saints" (Jude 3 NIV). He was preoccupied with defending and preaching the biblical faith, while others so often mocked it or ignored it. He learned to do battle face to face with those who hold error, and yet to do so graciously but very firmly. He was never seriously tempted to compromise for the sake of peace or to weaken when confronted with very charming and impressive liberals. He could see just how devastating error can be and how thin many liberal arguments are.

For John, as for many of us, his time at university was when his character and basic position were hammered out in the face of all sorts of alternative views. He had met head-on the fundamental challenges of the ruling liberal theology, but remained confident in the truth and spiritual power of the biblical faith.

5

"Please Do Not Disturb Unless Urgent"

MYRA CHAVE-JONES

Myra Chave-Jones was invited by John Stott in 1973 to set up a counseling and teaching service in central London that would offer psychotherapy from a distinctively Christian point of view. The service, named "Care and Counsel," continued until 1989. Author of several books in the field of Christian counseling, Myra died in 2010.

My first encounter with John was in 1941 when we were both students at Cambridge. I was struck, initially, by this gorgeous creature who, in his role as usher, drifted up and down the central aisle of Holy Trinity Church before the CICCU sermon on Sunday evenings. With his impressive undergraduate gown and his solemn but courteous demeanor, he caught everyone's attention.

I was looking forward to meeting him, therefore, when I was deputed to invite him to lead one of our college Bible readings. I crept up to his room with some trepidation. I was about to knock on his door when I spied a neat little typed notice saying:

8.00 am–8.00 pm working.
Please do not disturb unless urgent.

Leading Bible studies was obviously trivia, so I disappeared hastily, thinking, *What an extraordinary person!*

I used to see John in the university library from time to time. He always sat in the same place, used the same books and appeared totally oblivious of anything that was going on around him. I was later to discover that this ruthless self-discipline was a dominant feature of his life, and to some extent the secret of his success, but at the time I only thought how boring it must be!

Our contact in Cambridge was minimal, but subsequently I often heard of his developing influence in the evangelical world. It was not until years later that I found myself living very near All Souls Church. It was a tremendous privilege to learn from John's meticulously prepared and lucidly delivered sermons each Sunday. Again and again he made difficult subjects understandable. One of those sermons, in particular, created a remarkable turning point in my life.

In those days everyone had to address him as "Rector," but having known him previously, I was not about to be so formal. I still have a little note from him, allowing me to call him "John" when we were "in private conversation"! This was part of his policy to avoid anything that could remotely call into question his Christian integrity.

I remember being surprised by the very ordinary little car which he drove (too fast and too dangerously!). I had been used to people in positions of authority going about in Jaguars and the like. But ostentation was not part of John's Christian lifestyle.

I began to see more of John, and a strange relationship developed. He was always courteous, kind, generous and encouraging, but part of him was difficult to engage with. I must admit to having been a bit overawed by his erudition and influence; he on the

other hand often seemed to be opening doors and then shutting
them just as I was about to approach (which felt like a repeat of the
Cambridge experience). I was often reminded of *Alice in Wonder-
land* and the animals' dance:

> "Will you walk a little faster?"
>   said a whiting to a snail.
> "There's a porpoise close behind us,
>   and he's treading on my tail." . . .
> "Will you, won't you, will you,
>   won't you, will you join the dance?"

We were two inhibited people trying to meet. He often described
himself as "a cold fish." This was only partly true; it was just that
the warm-blooded fish was concealed under iron discipline!

I remember one occasion when he misinterpreted something I
said when we were at The Hookses. I had never seen him angry
before, and this was quite an eye-opener. I could feel the emotional heat coming from him, although he was not saying anything. He just walked away and wrestled with himself, leaving me
amazed. But within an hour he was his usual gracious and charming self (and cold fish!) again.

John was not always a good judge of character, I think. Perhaps
this was because, as an eternal optimist, he was always eager to
see the best in everyone, so at times his vision became a bit blurred.
Sometimes I was able to help him slightly in his role as pastor at
All Souls because I had some knowledge of psychotherapy. His
basic attitude at first was that "all this introspection is positively
pathological." But gradually he softened a bit.

It was mainly through his initiative that Care and Counsel was
established, a "counseling center" designed for people who were
struggling with emotional problems that were hindering their
spiritual and emotional growth. In those days Care and Counsel
was ahead of its time, breaking entirely new ground in the con-

ventional evangelical world, where the usual attitude was that "more prayer and Bible study would solve such problems." But many churches allowed me to talk to their pastoral teams about the implications of being human as well as being spiritual. I was riding unashamedly on John's back because the name John Stott would open most doors. Care and Counsel was in some ways a prototype of the Christian counseling centers and books that now abound on the topic. John's unfailing support in many ways was crucial to this breakthrough, even though it was not really his own special interest.

One time I tried to introduce him to a bit of culture to widen his interest from birds and the Bible. I took him to the National Gallery with all its treasures, where he listened to my expositions with polite and patient attention. Then I tried something else and took him to *Cats* (Andrew Lloyd Webber's famous musical based on T. S. Eliot's poems). John sat totally unmoved when one of the "cats" came and stroked his cheeks with its whiskers (he was probably thinking about the following day's sermon!). When I discovered that watching James Bond films was one of John's favorite pastimes, I finally gave up and concluded, probably very unfairly, that under his genteel façade he was really a bit of a philistine!

Often he would fail to reply to some request or suggestion of mine, and I would think that since he was such a saint, he had no business to behave in such a cavalier manner. But one day he said, "I expect you have been cursing and swearing at me." I was surprised and amused at such language from him, but by then we had reached a deep and loving relationship of trust, something that has remained ever since.

One of the things I respected about John was his ability to keep up with and respond to greatly changing attitudes in the church and wider society, while retaining his own theological position as an anchor in thinking through everything that confronted him.

John was one of the most Christlike people I have ever known.

His forbearance, patience, gentleness, genuine humility (in spite
of such widespread admiration) and a thousand other fruits of the
Spirit were well known to everyone and an abundant blessing to
all of us.

6

"IT TAKES JUST SEVEN
AND A HALF MINUTES"

TIMOTHY DUDLEY-SMITH

*Timothy Dudley-Smith was bishop of Thetford from 1981 to
1992 and also served as president of the Evangelical Alliance. A
prolific writer of hymns (including "Tell Out, My Soul"), he
wrote the major two-volume biography of his lifetime friend
John Stott, published by IVP. Since retirement, he lives near
Salisbury.*

My first memories of John Stott go back to Iwerne Minster in
April 1944. I was a schoolboy, and this was my first time at Iwerne.
I remember running down the stairs just as the camp secretary
(John) was coming up. We stopped to make way for each other.
"You must be Timothy Dudley-Smith," he said. I was astonished,
though looking back it was just what one would have expected
from John.

We met next at what was one of the turning points of my life,
just outside my college, Pembroke, in my first few days at Cambridge. John (or "Mr. Stott" as I called him until with some amusement he told me not to) was sailing past on his bike, going back to

Ridley Hall. He stopped and greeted me. "Are you going to the pre-terminal meetings of the Christian Union?" he asked. "The first is tonight in the Old Combination Room at Trinity." I looked blank and evasive. So John propped his bicycle against the college wall. "Do you know where Trinity OCR is?" he asked. "No," I said. "I'll walk you there now," he volunteered. "It takes just seven and a half minutes." Needless to say, that was exactly how long it took. We then walked back to Pembroke, where John collected his bike and cycled off with a cheerful, "See you there this evening!" I had no choice after that, and so began a link with CICCU that was decisive for my Cambridge years and, indeed, for my whole life and ministry.

There have been many other decisive moments since then, leading to lasting associations with him: when, for example, he invited me to be the founding editor of *Crusade* magazine (when he was chair of the Evangelical Alliance Literature Committee), and then the long association with him in the Eclectics Society (he invited me to the very first meeting), as a member of Christian Debate, then as a member of the Church of England Evangelical Council (and later co-chairman with John and a very poor substitute in his absence), and as a member of the Evangelical Literature Trust (now Langham Literature), to which all the income from his writings has been donated.

And of course there were many more personal moments. Before he left Ridley, he encouraged me to use his shelves as a lending library. A large part of the pleasure of exchanging one book for the next was the chance of meeting and talking with him, sometimes waiting while the day darkened until he returned so I could pour out my troubles. Much later, I once asked him by letter if he would supply a reference for me, to accompany my application for a full-time prison chaplaincy. He did not do so, but instead took the trouble to explain why he could not feel that this was the right next step for me, but asking me to pray further about it and think again. Only if I was then sure would he gladly be my referee. I did as he said and came to see my intended application as more of a romantic gesture of frustration than as a genuine call of God.

I recall my first visit to The Hookses over a New Year in the mid-1950s. We were a bachelor party. We laid tongue-and-groove flooring in the barn. Then we helped John build a blind on the cliff top from which he could watch gulls tear to pieces a poor dead rabbit, strategically pinned down in front of us. Ever since then, in response to John's enthusiasm for birds, I have reminded him (as I once did in the presence of a Royal Society for the Protection of Birds warden) that I really prefer my birds on a dish with gravy around them.

Other visits to The Hookses were usually to take part in "Dale Day"[1] or to research his biography. But from early on in his ministry, John used to come to our home about once a year and we would spend a day off together. When we were in Sevenoaks we would walk together in Knole Park and talk about whatever plans were in his mind: the All Souls Clubhouse, perhaps, or the Christian Foundations series of books, or the National Evangelical Anglican Congress at Keele. If he was still with us when our children came home from school, he was a very popular visitor. When we lived in Norfolk, we would take him to a nature reserve—Minsmere, perhaps, or out on the Broads. I remember him telling the warden of one of these sites that on his way in, he had just heard the distinctive notes of some bird that was a summer visitor to these shores. "Too early," the warden dismissed, "they've not arrived yet." "Just come back down the path fifty yards and listen," persisted John. And sure enough—you can guess the rest.

In company with all his friends and countless others to whom he is only a name, I owe much of my theological education to John's writings. As it happens, I was one of his early publishers, with the booklet *Fundamentalism and Evangelism* (Crusade, 1956). (*Men with a Message* had come out two years earlier, and *Basic*

Christianity arrived two years later.) That booklet brings to mind
the sense of relief I felt that John, already known as a pastor and
evangelist, was willing to become involved in controversy in de-
fense of the gospel. And this willingness has been amply confirmed ever since, of course, in books such as *Christ the Controversialist* (1970) and *Essentials,* his dialogue with David Edwards
(1988).

I recall walking around a farmer's field in East Anglia with
John, following a meeting of the Evangelical Literature Trust (ELT)
trustees, in which he unfolded to me the invitation he had received to do that dialogue with David Edwards. It caused me extreme misgivings. It seemed to me that there would be a kind of
"make-or-break" element in such a dialogue with an accomplished
liberal scholar and commentator, and I was not at all sure that I
wanted John to be involved in it. I was on holiday in Cornwall
with my family when, as he had promised, John sent me the manuscript to read. I begged off a day at the beach with the family, lay
in the garden in the sun and plunged in. Of course I was immediately cheered by David Edwards's description of John as being
"apart from William Temple . . . the most influential clergyman in
the Church of England during the twentieth century." But my
heart sank to read his cogent questioning of the evangelical position—only to rise again when I came to John's chapter-by-chapter
response. The book remains, in my view and in its own genre, a
tour de force of evangelical apologetics.

It was an immense and unexpected privilege for me to be invited
to be John Stott's biographer. It became my main preoccupation in
the first ten years of retirement from office. John allowed me to put
a note in his newsletter inviting contributions from his worldwide
circle of friends. But in the end, I could not use a fraction of the
letters that arrived, since so many of them said exactly the same
thing: "I feel I must write to tell you what a blessing John Stott's
preaching/writing/visits have been to me and my family. His Bible

teaching has served to ground us more firmly in the faith, and the example of his simple lifestyle, his personal humility and his evident love for Christ have been an inspiration to us."

As a friend of John, it was a joy to me to receive such letters, but as his biographer, after the first three or four, they began to pall! But I could well understand the desire of the writers to pay tribute to him.

Dear John! How much we owe him! How different my own ministry would have been if he had not stopped me on the stairs all those years ago and known my name! When I was researching for the biography in London, while he was abroad or at The Hookses, he would allow me to stay at his flat. As I browsed among his books and files, I often found myself thanking God for all he has been to so many people. It was fitting that his last Keswick address should have been on "Christlikeness," since he embodies that as much as anyone I have ever known. To visit him, as I have done, even in his old age and infirmity at the College of St. Barnabas, is to come away with a surer sense of the unseen world of spiritual reality. I find myself reminded again of the call to disciplined living, to biblical priorities and to faithful prayer. And it brings to mind the time I knelt with him in his study in Weymouth Street in the 1950s when the future of *Crusade* magazine hung in the balance, its finances precarious and my own position therefore unsure. As we prayed, John gave me a verse which I had never previously noticed in my reading, but have met so often since. Even in our eighties—as we both are at the time of my writing this—I like to think it still applies to both of us: "For I know the plans I have for you, declares the LORD, plans for welfare and not for evil, to give you a future and a hope" (Jeremiah 29:11 ESV).

HELPLESS WITH LAUGHTER
AT THE HOOKSES

DICK LUCAS

Dick Lucas was rector of St Helen's, Bishopsgate, from 1961 to 1981, and Rector Emeritus in his retirement. Author of several books, some based on his Keswick addresses, he founded the Proclamation Trust and Cornhill Training Course to foster strong biblical preaching and teaching.

I share some memories of John Stott, not so much of a great ministry as of a great friend, and a loyal one too. My first recollection of John is at the Iwerne camp in 1941. Aged fifteen, I was at camp only because in the holidays some form of farm work was expected. "Don't you know there's a war on?" stared down at us from billboards and was firmly repeated to anyone daring to hope for more than their minuscule ration of butter and sugar. John, an undergraduate at Cambridge at the time, was running the camp office in his tidy and efficient way, keeping the books, plotting trains and travel, chasing up enough food for the hungry hordes, as well as preventing disasters and detailing future plans. Of all this background work I knew nothing, of course, except that everything ran wonderfully smoothly. But I did hear a memorable evening talk from this rosy-cheeked leader. He spoke on the cross of Christ, and even back then his talk was accessible to all, and moving too.

It seems remarkable how often, over many years, I can recall hearing him speak on this wonderful theme of the cross, as for instance many years later at Haverfordwest Parish Church, on one of his favorite verses, Galatians 6:14, or at a great mission to Cambridge University, of which more later. Now, since the publication of his magnum opus on the cross of Christ, all who care to do so may benefit from his teaching. That is a book of which Dr. J. I. Packer has said, "No other treatment of this supreme subject says so much so truly and so well." It gives me much satisfaction and joy to note that, according to my replacement copy of 2003, the book had by then been reprinted fifteen times. May it continue to be reissued and read until Christ returns! Nobody should miss the magnificent section on the "self-substitution" of God. As a preacher, I know the treasure that is here, for written on the fly-leaf of my copy I find: "Read again during Holy Week while in Dublin for combined churches [meeting] 2004." How many speakers must have mined gold from the pages of this book!

John Stott was at the heart of three of four student missions at Cambridge University between 1949 and 1958, organized by the student Christian Union (the despised CICCU, treated often as its Master was: Isaiah 53:3). The three main missioners were strikingly different. Dr. Barnhouse in 1949 was massive in build, colorful in robes and language, strongly doctrinal like a Reformation father, uncompromising and confrontational. I had heard nothing like it, nor had the packed student congregation who, night by night, turned out in force to be dealt with most faithfully. Sincerity and frankness were Dr. Barnhouse's style; sin, righteousness and judgment were his staple themes. To my personal knowledge the fruit of that mission endures. Then, in 1955, Billy Graham, with John Stott as his chief assistant missioner, bravely and courteously faced the hostility of the educational establishment. And what a week that was! Surely comparable in significance to Moody's visit in November 1882.

So to John Stott himself, the main speaker for 1952 and 1958. Cambridge must, I think, have been taken aback that one of its own scholars, a "First" in theology, should be the chosen spokesman of the CICCU. The preaching was wonderful in its clarity, and the message was the old apostolic gospel of Jesus and his sacrificial love. Long queues reaching far down King's Parade bore witness to the attraction of the man, what he had to say and how he said it. Those Cambridge missions set standards for numerous university missions around the globe taken by John Stott in the following years.

Clarity, yes. But also exposition! To this day I recall something of the shape of an Oxford sermon of John's on 1 Timothy 2:3-7. He preached on "God Our Savior Who Wants *All* to Be Saved," explaining from the passage that there is *one God, creator of all, one Mediator, providing a sufficient ransom for all,* and *one message for all* (emphasis added), exemplified in Paul's missionary call. Since those days expository preaching has been high on the agenda among convinced evangelicals, and John Stott, more than anyone, has been responsible for this. An Australian friend frequently confirms to me the new impulse for expository work in the pulpit that followed John's early visits "down under."

Life at The Hookses demands a mention. I refer to the "olden days" when primitive conditions reigned in abandoned farm buildings, such as hard mattresses, bare boards and oil lamps that sent out black smoke when handled by the unskilled. There were no fences round the property then, and the local sheep roamed everywhere, impertinently eating the few flowers that had escaped the wild Atlantic storms and were being lovingly tended by the rector of All Souls. But what happy hours were spent there, famously commemorated by that budding poet Timothy Dudley-Smith. On my visits it became customary for me to take up residence in Helen's Hut, which I was glad to do—except in the middle of the night when nature called. Then, well wrapped up against the wind, torch in hand, I would tread carefully across two planks over a stream, then across the long wet grass in which legions of slugs conducted their amorous night exercises, finally to reach refuge in the men's washroom. They tell me that Helen's Hut is now "en-suite." I congratulate my successors, even if I cannot wholly approve such self-indulgence.

One key to life with John at The Hookses was to find some way of encouraging him to relax. This could only be for a while, of course, since he was there for sustained periods of writing (the fruit of which everyone knows in the string of fine commentaries and books), while we who came for a week or so were usually in a holiday mood. I used to hope, rather pessimistically, that some rare bird, unknown to the great man, might choose to lodge nearby for a while, which could mean that, with blinds erected and field glasses round his neck, John would willingly leave his desk for hours in order to scrutinize its every movement. Truthfully, on one occasion, a large green caterpillar of uncommon breed and lineage kept our host and his camera occupied for several days. In the afternoons, however, he would appear, not to relax but to recruit the more muscular of his guests for the task of laying concrete paths, dredging the pond or unblocking drains, while we of the weaker sort would depart for the delights of Marloes Beach, shopping at nearby St. David's, or if we were fortunate, discovering cream teas at a neighboring farm. The key to this last pleasure seemed to be that the muddier the ground, or the more desolate the wrecks of old tractors and scrapped car bodies, the better would be the teas. But best of all was being joined by John after supper, in the tiny sitting room, for a reading of old favorites, perhaps Saki's "The Lumber Room" or "The Story Teller," when, unfailingly, John would dissolve into helpless laughter over the wolf, whose "pale grey eyes gleamed with unspeakable ferocity" prior to devouring "to the last morsel," Bertha, the girl who was "horribly good."

Since Timothy Dudley-Smith's splendid two-volume biography of John Stott appeared, I am frequently accosted and asked about the book I was supposed to have written at The Hookses. The only reply I can give is that it must have been that exceptional rarity—a scheme of John's that did not come off.

At The Hookses, one seemed to leave all troubles and troublesome people behind. I've scratched my head to think of anything that disturbed the peace of days spent there, but without success. There was one occasion when a group of us was taken over to the island of Skomer for the afternoon. To show us a puffin, John lay on the ground in order to put his arm down a rabbit burrow where they build their nests. Immediately, he received a sharp nip for his efforts and drew out the black-and-white sea bird with the beautifully colored bill that sat on his finger, blinking in the light. Unluckily, just at the very moment when we were gazing at this sight with admiration, the Nature Reserve Warden came over the hill. He instantly assumed that we were a group of louts up to no good and delivered a thorough lashing with his tongue. It was embarrassing. I am sure the good man had no idea that our guide was a near neighbor and a gifted naturalist who probably knew more of the islands and their bird life than he did.

Most of what I have touched on happened forty and more years ago. Anglican evangelicals were a smaller company then than they are now, but far from ineffective, and generally united under the outstanding leadership of the young John Stott. If today such evangelicals are far more widespread, it is in large measure due to the foundations he helped to lay, both in the United Kingdom and worldwide.

As I write this, in a few days John will be coming to breakfast—

something we have often enjoyed together over the years. No one could be less demanding or more appreciative of the simplest fare provided, although we will do better than that in order to prepare him for yet another active day. His weakness is for chocolates, but that is not exactly suitable for a breakfast menu, though, on second thought, a chocolate croissant might be slipped in rather that the customary toast. On a desert island his luxury would surely be a monthly supply of the best Belgian chocolate from Waitrose. Of course I assume that a Bible and binoculars will already be there. And birds without number to welcome him.

ALL SOULS AND
THE WIDER CHURCH
OF ENGLAND

"I Would Not Wish to Have
Had Any Other Calling"

FRANCES WHITEHEAD

*Frances Whitehead grew up in South Devon but spent a few
years living abroad after the war (in Switzerland and then South
Africa), before returning to England in 1951 and coming to London soon afterward. In 1956 she became personal secretary to
John Stott and has remained so ever since, though she officially
"retired" in 2011.*

My memories of John go back a very long way! It was in April
1956 when he was in his mid-thirties that he appointed me as
church secretary of All Souls. In effect this meant that I became
his personal secretary, and I have had the privilege of remaining
as such ever since! However, my first encounter with him was in
the earlier 1950s when I was working at the BBC and was a very
nominal Christian.

Going for a stroll in my lunch hour one day, I heard church
bells ringing. Making my way toward them, I came upon St. Peter's Church, Vere Street. To my amazement, I found the church
full of people listening to a young clergyman preaching from a

text in the Bible. I could barely find a seat in a side aisle, but my interest was immediately aroused by the speaker's manner and bearing, and the clarity of his message. There was a compelling seriousness about this man and the way he was explaining the Scriptures. I was so intrigued by all that I saw and heard there that I began attending those lunch hour services regularly.

Later I started to attend Sunday services at All Souls, until the day came when I finally encountered the living Christ through John Stott's preaching one New Year's Eve. What I remember most of all that night, as he was explaining the story of Nicodemus, was his repeated exhortation: "Don't look at me; look at Christ." So, for the first time in my life, it seemed to me that I consciously "looked at Jesus," saw him in all his beauty and grace, and prayed to him to be my Savior. John's exhortation and evident longing that people would "look to Jesus" and yield their lives to him remained one of the hallmarks of his ministry over all the years that I have known him. Like many thousands of others, I know that under God I owe my salvation on the human level to John's faithful preaching—I am eternally grateful.

My first face-to-face meeting with John (or "Mr. Stott" as we ladies all had to call him in those days) was some months later when I had a personal interview with him. I wanted to know how to proceed in the new life of faith which I had discovered. Typically, John had a very tight schedule, and it turned out he only had fifteen minutes to spare, just before he was due to give a lecture in the church. But it was long enough for him to realize that I was a new Christian believer, so he invited me to a second interview and then duly ensured that I was integrated into the life of the church family. Several years later, to my amazement, he invited me to join the staff team, which in those days was composed mainly of young curates (assistant pastors) and just two of us in administrative roles.

One of the first things I discovered about my new boss was that he was exceedingly efficient. He had at his fingertips all the knowledge to pass on to me about how to handle a mass mailing to the congregation in the quickest possible way, how to stick stamps on at speed (but they must always be straight!), how to keep records of just about everything that went on in the church and how to produce work on time—always today and never tomorrow! It was because he himself worked so incredibly hard, never idle for a moment but always concerned supremely for the glory of God, that I too was motivated to try to keep up with him and to please God as well. He certainly always drove himself to the limit, and some (like my mother) regarded him as a "slave driver" and told him so. But anyone who has ever worked with him in any capacity will vouch for his total commitment to whatever cause he espoused, no matter what the cost.

In those early years John Stott may have seemed distant and unapproachable—living to a strict timetable with an endless list of tasks to be accomplished each day (never to be interrupted in his study unless in dire emergency!). But he wonderfully mellowed over the years, and increasingly he shared many matters with me. He would call the three of us (himself, myself and his study assistant) the "happy triumvirate," and he would allow us freely to express our opinions on much that concerned him. It was always important to him to seek consensus about any decision he had to make.

He was a gracious, truly humble man and a servant of others. It still amazes me that he emptied my office wastepaper basket every day for many, many years. He always wanted to encourage others and appreciate their efforts, seldom if ever criticizing or rebuking, and quick to forgive if anyone overstepped the mark. He had a particular love for children and would visibly soften as they shyly approached him. Then he would solemnly shake their hand and try to engage them in simple conversation.

John had amazing powers of concentration and, once absorbed

in a writing project or an issue requiring careful consideration, he
was totally oblivious to what was going on around him. Many is
the time that I have gone into the room needing to speak to him
and waited for him to realize that I was there. But it would not be
until I had made enough noise to attract his attention that he
would look up from his desk in surprise. Then he would hold his
head in his hands for about thirty seconds, murmuring, "You don't
know how painful it is—you don't know how painful it is," while
he obviously made the journey back from whatever subject had so
totally absorbed him into the mundane world of the present day.

On the lighter side of life, John had an amazing fund of jokes
and stories which he would produce at the drop of a hat, and he
loved to share his own knowledge of just about everything under
the sun with anyone who would listen. "I don't know" was not an
expression I was allowed to get away with—if I didn't know, then
I had to find out! And when it came to an unknown word or expression, out would come the *Oxford Dictionary* or *Brewer's Dictionary of Phrase and Fable*, and John would duly enlighten me!

Then there was his passion for accuracy or exactness. This was
not confined only to his own writing style or his preaching, but
was required of me when relaying a message to him—I had to get
the details right because he would inevitably ask all sorts of sup-
plementary questions as to how, when and why the message had
been left. John wanted all our work to be worthy of the Lord—and
that meant nothing could be sloppily done. Many is the letter I
completely retyped before presenting it to him for signature because I spotted a mistake somewhere along the line. Once, when I
had not checked a letter carefully, I suddenly heard John in fits of
laughter and rendered almost speechless because I had mistak-
enly typed in one of his letters to an elderly pastor: "I too am still
preaching although I am now 875 years old"!

Many will know that John believed in and practiced the simple
lifestyle, but not many will know, as an example of that commit-

ment, that at one time he only had one pair of suitable shoes to wear in London. When they needed repair, I would take them home at the weekend and get the local cobbler to do the job, while my mother would exclaim in amazement, "Surely that man can afford to have a second pair!" And what about buying clothes? John thoroughly disliked going shopping, regarding it as a waste of time. But when the inevitable moment came and he had to buy something new, he tended to take the first jacket or pair of trousers he tried on, regardless of fit, rather than spend time trying on anything more! Food shopping, however, was another matter, and in later years he regularly did most of his own. Once a week, early on a Saturday morning, he would walk down to the local supermarket in Marylebone High Street, go round with his cart, fill his shopping bags, and then come back in a taxi.

Over the years, I spent many working weeks with John down at The Hookses in Wales, usually accompanied by whoever was John's study assistant at the time. While John concentrated on his writing, I simply transferred "the office," as he called it, down there. Once installed, we followed a regular daily routine of work, interspersed with meals at set times, but when it came to Sunday we eased off a bit, donned tidier clothes, cleaned our shoes and were allowed breakfast just half an hour later than usual before going to church in Dale, the local village. John's love of nature was most evident when he was at The Hookses, and somehow his amazing powers of concentration never seemed to prevent him from spotting some unusual bird that had just landed on the cliff opposite his study window. Then he would stop what he was doing, call for me to get my binoculars and go and have a look!

Everything about The Hookses and its environs gave him immense pleasure, but he was always distressed if he saw the nearby hedgerows or gorse bushes defaced by discarded rubbish, for it was "God's garden" to be cherished. I have vivid memories of an occasion when, on our way back from the Sunday morning church service, John suggested that I drive the car slowly up the long lane leading to the airfield, while he and a friend got out, each with a black bin liner in hand, and proceeded to walk behind the car, picking up all the rubbish on the way—empty cigarette boxes, empty bottles and cans, plastic bags in abundance and large agricultural sacks that must have blown over the hedges from the fields alongside. By the time we reached the gate at the top, both bags were full and John was satisfied!

John was very generous, both with his money and his time. His desire was always to be positive and to help anyone in genuine need. He would go to endless lengths to assist and minister to them, whether they were friends or complete strangers, and he always had a special care for widows and orphans. I was touched by his special care for me when I reached my eightieth birthday. He took it upon himself, unknown to me, to get in touch with a few of my friends and then with them personally to lay on a celebration lunch. He later arranged for me to go to Brussels with a friend for five days. He even went to the length of coming to see us off at Waterloo Station on the Eurostar train, and handing each of us a fat packet of euros so that we could "treat each other" while we were away! He was marvelous at thinking through every conceivable detail of anything he chose to organize, even when well on in his eighties!

As I look back over the years I can say without hesitation that my earliest impressions of John as a man of the utmost integrity have proved abundantly true. He was not only a brilliant Bible expositor but also one who sought constantly to live out what he believed and taught. He was a man of deep convictions and total commitment, and there was no dichotomy between faith and practice. He lived to serve and please God, to bring glory to his name and to boast in nothing but the cross of Jesus Christ. He rarely, if ever, talked about himself.

I found John to be a true friend and a great man to work for and with. I don't pretend that there were never times of exhaustion or tension between my commitment to him as his secretary and my desire for time to do other things! Outside activities frequently got squeezed out, but if I were to live my life all over again, I would not wish to have had any other calling, for the rewards have far outweighed the cost. It has been a tremendous joy to have had some small share in John's wide-ranging ministry and the blessing that has flowed from it to countless thousands of others worldwide.

9

A Curate in Need of Restraint

TED SCHRODER

*Ted Schroder was a curate at All Souls from 1967 to 1971, and
also chaplain to the Polytechnic of Central London, now the
University of Westminster. He was the founding president of the
Langham Foundation in the United States (which later became
John Stott Ministries, and then Langham Partnership USA). He
is now pastor at Amelia Plantation Chapel, Amelia Island,
Florida.*

One of my first unforgettable memories of John, after moving
into the rectory, was the prayer meeting he used to lead on Saturday nights. Half a dozen of us on the staff would crowd into his
study, along with one or two of his friends, such as Alec Motyer,
who at that time was vicar of a church in Hampstead. We would
all kneel and John would begin our prayer time. What left a lasting
impression on me was the way in which this great man, who inspired such admiration and, indeed, not a little awe, began his
prayer. He would echo the words of Abraham: "Now that I have
been so bold as to speak to the Lord, though I am nothing but dust
and ashes" (Genesis 18:27 NIV). If this celebrated preacher approached the Lord in such a humble and self-effacing way, who

was I to blurt out my requests discourteously? It set an example that has influenced my praying ever since.

It was well known that John and I had very different personalities, which came out in various ways. He was a reserved Englishman of the old-school-tie type. I was an ebullient Kiwi who never left a thought unsaid. Once, when I was preparing to process with John into All Souls, at a service in which I was to preach, I said to him, "John, I am praying for liberty." John replied, "And I am praying for restraint!" I have learned over the years the virtue of that prayer of his.

On another occasion, after I had preached passionately about some issue and tried to make my point, and hammered it home so that there would be no shadow of doubt, he said to me, "Ted, guard your flanks." I was so focused on the truth I was proclaiming that I didn't realize I had left myself open to the criticism of being unbalanced. He helped me to take into consideration other legitimate points of view and to incorporate them in my preaching so that the sermon became a dialogue with the questions being raised in the minds of the hearers, and therefore gained more credibility.

"I HAVE GOT MY SINS,
YOU HAVE GOT YOURS"

JOHN SMITH

*John Smith lived for five years as one of several residents at the
All Souls Rectory. He worked as Student Adviser at polytechnics
in London and then as Head of Student Services at Bristol Polytechnic until his retirement in 1996. He continues to live in
Bristol.*

I was fortunate to serve most of my National Service days with
a former All Souls choirboy, Peter Challand. For one of our two
years, our unit was based in Devonshire Street, almost directly
opposite the entrance to Bridford Mews. After our demobilization
in 1956, my friend had been invited by John Stott to a choir supper. Peter was so overwhelmed by John's welcome and his accurate
recollections of Peter's boyhood, that he told me he would very
much like to attend services at All Souls again, but felt apprehen-
sive about going by himself.

Since I had been a regular churchgoer from an early age, I volunteered to accompany Peter to the Sunday morning services, so
in the spring of 1957, we found ourselves at an All Souls Guest

Service, and following a challenging sermon, we walked to the front to meet John. For me, this was symbolic of Christian commitment. A few days later I received an invitation to an "At Home" at the rectory.

John was then thirty-six, and meeting him for the second time, his firm handshake, those penetrating blue eyes and his engaging manner were just as striking as on the previous occasion at All Souls. I still marvel at the exchange that took place between us at the end of our meeting, in the hallway of 12 Weymouth Street. I had asked John if I could speak with him on some personal matter, and we both consulted our Filofax diaries to arrange a mutually convenient time. My somewhat unreasonable mental approach was, *When can I fit this in?* John, on the other hand, gave me the impression that he could see me almost any time, at my convenience. The reality, as I soon learned, was that his diary probably had a dozen more entries per day than mine, and while I would have had at least three or four free evenings a week, he would have had none. Simply put, he was so humble, patient, accommodating and accepting.

I had been assigned to John (Des) Dugan at the "At Home," and his role, in current parlance, was to disciple me. Des was then John's PA and bursar at All Souls, and a resident at "the Wreckage" (some former residents' designation for 12 Weymouth Street—a combination of rectory and vicarage). Des became a "godfather" to me and was very generous in inviting me to countless meals at the rectory, where John Stott lived and worked. Through these regular invitations from Des, I got to know John better, and in the summer of 1963 he invited me to become a resident at No. 12. This period of living with John lasted for five years and was a time of privileged learning and growth.

For four of the five years, my bedroom was immediately under John's. With the creaking floorboards of a period terraced house, I invariably heard John going to bed and also getting up each day.

Rarely did he sleep for a full six hours, and sometimes even less. Then in his mid-forties, John regularly took a half-hour nap after lunch, as he had been doing for many years already, to recharge and increase his output. His wake-up ritual was to fill his lungs with fresh air at his open bedroom window and take a cold bath—which practice he told me he stopped at the age of fifty. These demonstrations of self-discipline have continued throughout his life, and even as recently as March 2008 he told me he continued his fast from chocolate during Lent to demonstrate to himself that he was still in control of his body.

Occasionally, on his way from his study to his bedroom, if my light was still on, he would stop off to raise some issue, particularly after I had taken over managing the rectory accounts. His visits were always brief. On one occasion he inquired of me how seriously I was courting a young lady whom he knew very well and with whom he had often seen me talking on the steps of All Souls. "I am not courting her at all," I protested. "Very well then," said John, "but does she know that?"

There were many interesting discussions around the meal table. One in particular stands out, on the evening following the meeting at the Central Hall, Westminster, in October 1966, when the hugely controversial question of whether evangelicals should "come out" of mainstream denominations was debated. Martyn Lloyd-Jones argued passionately that they should, while John Stott disagreed. I recall David Wells, the now well-known scholar and author, expressing the view that John had abused his role as chairman. Maybe this dinner table exchange contributed to John later making an apology to Martyn Lloyd-Jones.

Over the past fifty years I have spent many separate weeks with John and others at The Hookses, where John was always at his most relaxed. On my first visit in 1960, with Martin Peppiatt leading a Wednesday Club party,[1] John escorted the group to Skomer, the birdwatchers' island paradise. He was at pains to provide us with some practical ornithology. While John had his arm down an old rabbit burrow trying to find and show us a puffin chick, I cheekily and impulsively asked, "Did anyone hear that lesser-speckled twitch warbler?" (or some such nonsense). "No," was John's immediate response, "but I did hear that long brown-haired babbler." John was superb at the "put down," but always with good grace.

John was an ardent lover and public reader of the writer Saki. Many a party at The Hookses has listened to him reading a chapter or two, sometimes with tears rolling down his cheeks and convulsed in laughter. The Wednesday Club members were receptive listeners. John was a great raconteur and storyteller. I have listened to some of his stories again and again, and two of them stand out because he was so good at mimicking accents, both from the time he was curate at All Souls.

On one occasion back in the 1940s, the then verger, Mr. Denham, took John aside and told him how he and his wife thought that one of the other staff members at All Souls was "a ladies' man." John adds that the person in question was a very smart and handsome young man and surely left behind him a trail of disappointed young ladies with bleeding hearts! Mr. Denham, as the story goes, then confided to John in an impeccable cockney accent, "But me and Mrs. Denham, we says, you ain't!"

The other story concerns John being asked by Mr. Earnshaw-Smith, the previous rector, to form a youth club. This John did. He also started a football team, which played in Regent's Park. One year the team played twelve games and won twelve! Another year, however, there was a boy who was particularly troublesome. John's solution to reform this young character was to make him captain of the team. In his first game as captain, there emerged another annoying member of the team who insisted on shouting to team members how they should play. After a while the new captain could stand this no longer, so he asked the referee (John) to stop the game. Then he yelled out to the usurper, "Why don't you shut your moaning 'ole up?!" John once concluded a letter from The Hookses to my wife, Anna, and me with a final line, "Now I'll shut my moaning 'ole up."

Anna and I have enjoyed several holidays with John at The Hookses. Some of these included such fun characters as Richard Bewes, Jonathan Fletcher and Dick Lucas. We all enjoyed one pre-dinner occasion when Dick Lucas, acting as a media interviewer, questioned Richard Bewes, who convincingly impersonated both Billy Graham and Luis Palau. The subject was John Stott, rector of All Souls Church, London, and Billy and Luis told us what they thought of the said gentleman!

John had a phenomenal memory. During the summer of 2006, he and I together affixed slate nameplates on all the residential buildings at The Hookses. We also hung and rehung pictures, photographs and artifacts in the new extension and in the older buildings. Although these items had been given to or obtained by John over a period of more than fifty years, he could remember the donor or the circumstances of acquisition in every case. Even at the age of eighty-five, his memory for Scripture references had hardly diminished. When I mentioned to him at The Hookses how I had copied out for our sons, Matthew and Nathan, the list of God's promises as printed in John's book *Your Confirmation*, he invited me to test him on them. He scored at least 90 percent in remembering accurately the wording of the sixteen biblical references!

Anna and I have listened to many of John's sermons and been nourished by them, just as we have learned much from his books. However, John was not only an amazing speaker and author, exercising great influence here in the United Kingdom and overseas through his university missions, over fifty books, and many strategic leadership positions. For us he has preeminently been a caring and loving pastor. Having married us in 1974, for several years thereafter he would telephone us on the right date to wish us a happy anniversary. He later remembered our twenty-fifth and thirtieth anniversaries. I have heard of many similar situations where John, through his incredibly organized diary-keeping, has telephoned friends on their birthdays or on the anniversary of the death of a spouse.

John led mostly by example, but he could also be very direct, as some of his former curates will recall. Once, when I had complained to John about what I had thought to be unacceptable behavior on his part, his response was, "Well Johnny, I have got my sins, you have got yours and the countess has hers. Now let's all get to bed!"

John took a genuine interest in our two sons, as he did with hundreds of his friends' offspring—witness the many family photographs in The Hookses photograph albums. Our son Matthew spent three formative years as John's study assistant, and this coincided with the beginning of John's physical decline. Effectively, therefore, Matthew became John's caregiver, especially during the last of these three years. In spite of their disparate years, the two of them developed a very close, loving relationship, which lasted beyond the years of Matthew's official role.

When John left this earthly life, there was a huge admixture of sadness and rejoicing, for he was a person, a preacher and a pastor extraordinaire.

11

"I WANT YOU TO TAKE OVER
FROM ME AT ALL SOULS"

MICHAEL BAUGHEN

Michael Baughen, formerly rector of Holy Trinity, Platt, Manchester, was asked by John to take over the helm of All Souls in December 1970, first (for legal reasons) as vicar, then rector; he was bishop of Chester from 1982 until his retirement in 1996. He cooperated with Timothy Dudley-Smith in composing tunes for some of his hymns and pioneered new paths in church music, including Youth Praise, Psalm Praise *and* Hymns for Today's Church.

I sat down in the chair. John Stott had asked me to come and see him next time I was in London. Now, on my way to a final rehearsal for the launch of *Youth Praise II* in the Royal Albert Hall, I had called in at the rectory, as requested, and was sitting opposite John in his study. I waited to hear what he wanted to talk to me about. John had always been flowing with innovative ideas and was determined to see them fulfilled in action. He had also shown that even mountains could not stop him. He either worked for their removal or went round them altogether. I assumed that there was another new idea in his mind, but had no clue what it was about.

John had become a guru for evangelicals in the Church of England and especially for the younger generation of ministers. He was clearly raised up by God as a pioneer leader. He saw that the advance of the gospel was being held back by traditional thinking and by the feeling evangelicals had in the 1950s that they were "in the corner and on the ropes." Only 10 percent of ordained pastors in the Church of England seemed to be of that theological persuasion, and their influence was confined to parochial evangelical ministries around the country—often very fruitful, but not affecting the church at large. There were all sorts of rules and shibboleths about liturgy (not a jot or tittle of the Prayer Book could be changed), clergy dress (even the size of collars!), negative commandments about the cinema or dancing or women wearing trousers, and the like. Any suspicion that a minister had strayed an inch from this narrow path could mean his being labeled "liberal" and pushed to one side. So many good men were deflected. Newly ordained evangelical ministers in the 1950s with a fervor for the gospel found much evangelical practice stifling, not to mention what they felt about the rest of the church!

Just as for Old Testament Israel in exile, a prophet was needed to bring evangelicals back to their basic roots and to rebuild their understanding of church. John's book *One People*, for instance, was exciting new thinking about church. Yet the most effective step he took was to call together a group of ministers, all under the age of forty, like himself, who would meet privately. The basic rule was that there was an acceptance of the authority of Scripture as the foundation for all discussion, but after that we were free to challenge and look freshly at everything. John called the group the Eclectics Society.

My first visit to an Eclectics day conference was so liberating and exciting that I felt I was driving home eighteen inches off the road afterward! The subject of the day was "Sunday." I had felt strangled in ministry by utterly negative thinking on that theme, with disastrous results at weekend youth camps. So to go back to Scripture and see what was actually said was like fresh air blowing through my mind and heart. John chaired the meeting, and when he said something I would scribble it down. Then someone challenged him. He pointed to another passage of Scripture that effectively queried what John had said. I drew my breath. You did not dare do that to gurus or leading evangelicals in those days. So it was thrilling when John looked at the passage and agreed that the point was well made and he had been wrong. This was truly letting Scripture be authoritative. It was liberating, affirming and just wonderful!

The original Eclectics meeting soon had to be repeated, and other groups began to spring up all over the country, with well-attended meetings and an exciting national residential conference each year. All sorts of new initiatives were started and developed: for example, writing, church structures, youth work, social concern and music. Once despised as nonacademic, evangelicals were flexing their academic and scholarly muscles. In the realm of worship, John encouraged the publication of *Youth Praise* in 1966, which rapidly revolutionized the singing of Christian youth groups across Britain and beyond.

Then came the planning for a major congress over several days at Keele University. The planning was done with older evangelical "fathers," who were for the most part godly and faithful men, but not yet affected by the new thinking that was changing the younger ones. The older way at such congresses was to give papers from the platform to a respectful passive audience. Eclectics wanted change. Some of the fathers met with John Stott and others of us in Eclectics leadership at an Eclectics Conference. And in a memorable "exchange of views" (as they say), John pleaded (or to be more accurate, demanded) on our behalf that papers should be published beforehand, and that the congress should discuss and make resolutions and decisions for action. The atmosphere in the room was almost one of open rebellion. Either the mountain would move or we would go round it. The mountain moved. The result was the Keele Congress of 1967, with all papers published beforehand. It brought all the new thinking into the main arena and began the development of Anglican evangelicalism into a growing, effective, influential and dynamic movement. This eventually resulted in a huge sea change in evangelical thinking and, consequently, in the whole Church of England.

John chaired the Keele Congress with consummate skill, working all hours with his team on the framing of resolutions. Outsiders at the congress rapidly observed what was happening and welcomed it. They could see that the theological fundamentals were being reinforced, but that there was a willingness to face the winds of change, to resist imposing a party line, and to move into wider fields such as social ethics and the social application of the Christian faith, areas that had been neglected by evangelicals for far too long. They also saw a move toward evangelicals taking a more responsible part in the life of the whole church. The Congress Statement also opened up structures of the church, worship forms, ministry, mission, international concerns, ecumenism and so much more. The whole face of the church would go on changing as a result, as history has proved.

So what, then, was in John's mind in 1969, two years after Keele, as I now sat waiting in front of him in his study? John is never one for small talk or introductions. His first words were breathtaking: "I want you to take over from me at All Souls."

It was so unexpected and so seemingly impossible a task that I was utterly stunned. John went on to explain the reason. He was traveling so much around the world that it was becoming increasingly difficult to exercise ministry as rector of the church. As soon as he would return home from some overseas trip, he would be inundated with requests, decisions, queries and complaints. If he was to fulfill his worldwide ministry and his writing, then he had to withdraw from the rectorship and have someone else take over. Such an idea raised all kinds of questions. How could it be done in the Church of England system of appointments? How would it work out in practice, even if it could be achieved? But for John, these were issues in the background. He was convinced it was right, and the mountains would have to be moved or bypassed.

I somehow managed to say to John that, as a railway enthusiast, the signals seemed at red, or at the very most a single yellow (which in the United Kingdom means that the track is clear only as far as the next signal). Frances Whitehead, John's wonderful secretary, drove me in her car to the rehearsal center. My head was spinning, my heart was in turmoil and my mind was saying no! But Frances warmly persisted in encouraging a yes! Then, a few weeks later, John was at the launch of *Youth Praise II* and afterward sent me a telegram: "Let the signals turn to green." John was always determined to see possibilities become actualities!

When I returned to Manchester and shared what had been said with my wife, Myrtle, we were in a turmoil of mind. We loved the ministry at Holy Trinity Church, Platt, and it was difficult to think that this move to London might be right for All Souls or for Platt or for our young family. Over the next months John worked on moving mountains, and was helped to do so with enthusiasm by the bishop of London and the archdeacon of London. If John were to resign, there was no guarantee at all that the Crown (patron of All Souls, with the right to appoint the rector) would invite me to take over as rector. If I went as an associate rector, the problem of ultimate authority in the church would not be overcome. So the idea was put forward that I could be made vicar and could take over the whole of the rectorial responsibility except the signing of legal papers. John would basically vacate the office of rector. Leadership of the church and its staff team, chairing of the parochial church council, and so on, would be handed over to me as vicar. John insisted that he would not intervene to overrule decisions and actions of the vicar if this plan proceeded. Looking back, it was an act of great daring by John. Eventually, after John had traveled north with yet more persuasion, Myrtle and I said a tremulous yes, but the lights were still at two yellows and did not turn to green until we had been a year at All Souls.

Most observers thought it would not work. But they had not accounted for John's determination to *make* it work. John did as he promised and totally vacated his rectorial office. Technically he remained rector until 1975 but effectively ceased in December 1970. He utterly refused to hear any complaints from parishioners whenever he returned to London from overseas. On one occasion, after a year, an anonymous letter was delivered, claiming to be from a large part of the congregation, demanding my resignation. But John stood shoulder to shoulder with us and the letter actually produced the reverse of its intent, with most of the congregation swinging into a new attitude of wonderful support. The church members also saw John enthusing about the changes in services, in music and in buildings. He always attended the church prayer meeting when in London. He was 100 percent behind the rebuilding of All Souls in 1975. Finally, it was during 1975 that indications were made that he could safely resign, and I was officially appointed rector. John became Rector Emeritus and was licensed to me as a curate. I was supposed to pay him a nominal £5 a year, but he delights to say that I failed to do so!

John became the dearest of friends and also a beloved "uncle" to our children. As he has done for thousands of others, he has prayed constantly for us and always encouraged us. Even when, in later years, I have stopped him (or tried to stop him!) going round what he thought was a mountain, it has not shaken our friendship.

John's amazing memory for people's names and his constant prayer and love for thousands has matched his brilliant scholarship, writing and strategic vision. Like the apostle Paul, he has been utterly faithful to that for which Christ called him.

12

"Nothing Can Go Wrong; John Stott Is Here"

RICHARD BEWES

Richard Bewes, the second son of CMS missionaries Cecil and Sylvia Bewes, had Kenya as his first home. He followed Michael Baughen as rector of All Souls from 1983 to 2004. Now retired in West London, he maintains a speaking, writing and broadcasting ministry.

I first met John Stott when I was thirteen years old. We, as a missionary family, had just returned from Kenya, and my father, Cecil Bewes, had taken a temporary position in Cornwall, so that we could have a holiday near the sea. John Stott, David Trapnell and another friend were camping in a nearby field. From time to time the three would come into the vicarage where we were staying for respite from the weather and vagaries of the country. It was in that summer that I was to attend my first "Bash Camp" at Iwerne Minster (where I would make my teenage commitment to Jesus Christ), and it was agreed that John would drive my younger brother Michael and me to Iwerne in his jeep.

That journey and camp became the start of a long association and friendship with John. When I went up to Emmanuel College, Cambridge, I would see John when he came to speak at CICCU events, and he always recognized me, addressing me by name. I remember buying books at the Scripture Union bookshop in Wigmore Street, London, and how he would sometimes greet me there with a playful punch in the stomach.

John's visits to Cambridge were always a highlight in the life of the CICCU. In 1955 he was chief assistant missioner alongside Billy Graham in the remarkable mission of that year. I was then on the executive committee of the CICCU, and it was a formative time for us all. Earlier, in 1954, John had been fully involved in the Billy Graham Harringay Crusade, attending every night of the three-month campaign. "The people were spellbound," he told me years later. I remember how John then came as the main speaker for the CICCU mission in 1958. Holy Trinity Church was packed night after night for his addresses. Many scores of students professed faith.

Later, when I was a curate at Christ Church, Beckenham, under Herbert Cragg, John seemed to many to be an iconic figure who could do no wrong. I joined the Eclectics Society, which he had founded for Anglican clergy under the age of forty. In those days John seemed to be everywhere—at Eclectics, at Diocesan Evangelical Fellowships, at conferences, consultations and missions. He was a formidable presence. Weak or unconsidered questions in public did not go down well with him.

When I was vicar of St. Peter's, Harold Wood, in London (1965-1974), I was struggling with how to deal with charismatic issues. I found both clarity and comfort in the letter that John wrote to me in his own hand. He was the anchor man for hundreds of us. There would always be something of a carnival spirit of expectation when he came to preach for us—as he also did at Emmanuel Church, Northwood, a decade later.

John continued to be held in very high regard by Billy Graham.

Evidence of this surfaced at Eurofest, a Bible youth event sponsored by Billy Graham Evangelistic Association in Brussels, in 1975. I was program chairman, and we expected that the highlight among all the sessions would be the one on "Leadership" to be led by John. However, before breakfast on the morning in question, Billy Graham phoned me in my hotel room. "I'm concerned," he said, "that John Stott has been assigned only one of several optional seminars to speak at. A man of his stature needs to be heard by us all. Would you mind if, at the close of the plenary Bible study this morning, I announce that the John Stott session is also to be plenary, and that I will chair it myself?"

I agreed of course (what else could you do with Billy Graham at the other end of the line?), and the announcement was duly made. "And," added Billy, "I want to make sure you all come with a notebook and pen. I too will be coming with my own notebook and my pen!" And sure enough he did, scribbling notes throughout the talk, and whispering urgently for more paper as his own supply ran out. It was very clear at that event, and in many other congresses, including Amsterdam and Lausanne, that Billy Graham and John Stott together were weaving a worldwide network of truth and trust among Bible believers everywhere.

"John, we had a great session with Sammy Escobar this morning!" I found myself enthusing from the back of the car. John was driving and we were taking a break in the countryside surrounding Lausanne during the epoch-making first Lausanne Congress on World Evangelization in 1974. Michael Baughen was beside me, and Misaeri Kauma (not yet a Ugandan bishop) was in the front passenger seat. John had not been present at the meeting. So, as he inevitably did when hearing a positive account of any gathering, he duly inquired, "And what were the particular emphases that Sammy was making?" I dug poor Michael Baughen in the ribs. "Go on, Michael, you tell him!"

I was appointed rector of All Souls Church in 1983. On the

morning of my institution on January 12, I found on my study desk a Staffordshire pottery figure of the renowned preacher, C. H. Spurgeon, with a little note attached from John. It has stayed with me ever since as a reminder of the strong bonds of fellowship generated between fellow preachers.

Not that I considered myself to be a preacher at all beside John. To begin with, despite our long friendship, I was fairly intimidated by his presence on the preaching team. "No, you mustn't think that" was his gentle reassurance when I voiced this anxiety to him. Our habit, instigated by him, of having coffee and prayer together every Saturday night helped to dissipate my qualms. And there was a psychological advantage in having John on the team and regularly sitting on the staff bench in the chancel. In a big central London church like All Souls, there is no guaranteed protection against the entry of extremists, exhibitionists or the deranged. But I would look over at John and think to myself, *Nothing can go wrong; John Stott is here!*

John gained something of a reputation for wishing to disagree with the title of a sermon or address that he had been assigned when it seemed to bear little relationship to the biblical passage in question. One spring, we were preaching our way through a series of sermons on the book of Deuteronomy, and he was due to expound a passage under the title "The Key to the Good Life." A note was passed under my door. "I would be grateful," it read, "if someone would be kind enough to explain to me what is meant by 'The Good Life,' and where in the passage I am expected to find this elusive key."

His worldwide reach was remarkable. True, I was rector of All Souls, but for many of our visitors it was John Stott whom they knew—or whom they *thought* they knew! "I'll never forget you," an Australian woman glowed to me one Sunday night on her way out of church, "or your wonderful visit to us in Melbourne in 1959!" (one of John's many trips to Australia). I had to let it go.

"Bless you!" I exclaimed, as I shook her hand.

"I've just bought a copy of *Basic Christianity*," an American exulted at the close of a service. "That's a marvelous book!" I acknowledged. "Well, thank you for writing it!" came the response. I had no option at that point but to declare my identity and put the credit where it really belonged.

"I've just bought a copy of *Basic Christianity*," beamed a Korean. "Now I want you to autograph it for me!" "Well," I hesitated, "if the author John Stott himself were here, I know that he *would* autograph it for you. But I'm not sure *I'm* the person who should be autographing it, are you?" The man's face fell for a moment. Then, rallying, he flashed his smile again. "I still want *you* to autograph it!" And I did.

The legendary tidiness and order of John's life was brought home to me once when he and I were both speakers at the Keswick Convention, staying in the Castlerigg Manor Hotel for the week. I was talking to the hotel staff member who had come to clean my room. I learned from her that she had been attending the convention.

"And how have you found the meetings?" I wanted to know.

"Well," came the reply. "I hear a good deal of how people have liked hearing one speaker and then another. But I judge these men not by their speeches, but by their bedrooms!"

"And on that basis," I hazarded, "who in your opinion is the outstanding speaker at Keswick this year?"

"Oh," she exclaimed, "there's absolutely no doubt about it—it's John Stott!"

"DRAGGED SCREAMING INTO THE MODERN WORLD"

DAVID TURNER

David Turner is a circuit judge, chancellor of the diocese of Chester and reader at All Souls Church, of which he has been a member since his student days. He was churchwarden there for twenty-three years until 2006. He has been a member of John's advisory group, the Accountability/Advisory Group of Elders (AGE), and worked closely with him over the years. He and his wife, Jean, live in London.

Whenever a human being, Bible in hand, stands up before a group of other human beings, invites the gathered assembly into a particular text of the Bible and as faithfully as possible tries to say again what the living God is saying in the text, something always happens. Something transformative, empowering, life-giving happens. . . .

It is the glory of preaching.

So Darrell Johnson of Regent College, Vancouver, begins the prologue to his fine book *The Glory of Preaching*.[1] John Stott would thoroughly approve!

It was as a preacher that John first made a direct impact on me when I arrived at All Souls in the autumn term of 1972. I had read some of his books before and often heard others speak appreciatively of him, but the impact on me, as a fairly new Christian and law undergraduate, of seeing and hearing him in the pulpit was immense and unforgettable. His patrician good looks, his lean frame and ruddy complexion, his (to my Northern Irish ears) precision and elegance of delivery were matched by the visual impact of his scarlet Queen's Chaplain cassock and gleaming surplice (lovingly ironed by some of the admiring women of the congregation, whom I would later hear him term affectionately "the Langham Ladies"!). I had never before seen any minister kneel in the pulpit immediately before he preached—as was then John's practice. This was someone who meant business. I had never heard preaching of such authority or clarity. I could not get enough of it.

It was very soon clear to me, even then, that John Stott's passion for the gospel, along with his visionary leadership, pastoral flair and preaching competence, had, under God, largely shaped the remarkable church family of All Souls—the church that he had continuously served since December 1945 and which has now been my own spiritual home for almost forty years. Three superb rectors have built on his foundations and relished his unfailing encouragement since. His loyalty to and immersion in the life of a single congregation have themselves been truly inspirational—a local pastor with a global ministry.

Little did I think in those early days that there would be opportunities to get to know and work with John, and, as the years passed, to come to know and love him as a brother and father in God. This is not a moment for detached objectivity. The John I have come to know is a remarkable, at times enigmatic, blend of passion and balance, humility and authority, scholarship and simplicity, austerity and warmth. As well as being the preacher and the pastor, he has been the visionary, the diplomat, the entrepreneur, the strategist, the intellectual, the writer, the communicator, the controversialist, the fundraiser, the friend. He has, to quote David Wells, at times "seen what others cannot see . . . and known how to get there." But, Wells continues, "Such are the qualities of integrity, love and wisdom that one finds in him that his leadership has always rested lightly on those around him."[2]

John's lifelong preoccupation, his "supreme concern" (as he himself put it in his customary prayer before preaching), has been Christ and "his greater glory." It is no exaggeration to say that John is probably the finest man I have ever known. No human being has overall influenced or inspired me more. My debt to him is incalculable.

Above everything else, John has helped me supremely in the areas of *thought* and *work:* the Christian *mind* and Christian *vocation.*

Paul speaks of the renewal of our minds (Romans 12:1-4). And John Stott had a passion for precisely the same vision. What Alister McGrath has termed "discipleship of the mind . . . the reshaping and recalibration of our ways of thinking in accordance with the patterns of reality disclosed in Christ"[3] mattered supremely to John. That "*the Bible* speaks today" was my developing conviction and weekly experience as I listened to his preaching. Here was communication of captivating relevance and power. But that newspapers, novels, films, even law reports could also all be rich material for "double listening" (as John liked to term his approach to "hearing" the word and the world)—that was something new and exciting to me. Evangelicals could have—must have—well-stocked minds, unafraid to think and to face difficult questions! That discovery was a wonderful personal liberation. Suddenly everything I read, viewed, thought, struggled with, could be brought to Scripture to seek "the mind of Christ." Mark Noll has put it well:

The effort to think like a Christian is . . . an effort to take seriously *the sovereignty of God* over the world he created, *the lordship of Christ* over the world he died to redeem and *the power of the Holy Spirit* over the world he sustains each and every moment. From this perspective the search for a mind that truly thinks like a Christian takes on ultimate significance, because the search for a Christian mind is not, in the end, a search for the mind but a search for God.[4]

John Stott made that effort and inspired others like me to do the same.

So much of John's time was spent making this process a reality. He established a reading group to which I belonged. We read novels, watched films, scanned magazines and tried to unpick their assumptions and worldviews. We read Castaneda and Fowles, Pirsig and Potok, Golding, Roszak, and dozens of others. We wrestled with *Cosmopolitan* magazine. We found ourselves cringing with embarrassment at some *risqué* film and standing baffled at the Tate gallery while one of our number enthused about Mark Rothko's *Black on Maroon*. These were great times. John savored the company of relaxed, talkative, young professionals, as many of us were. There was much laughter and occasional irreverent mimicry. John would later claim in print we had "dragged him screaming into the modern world," but, in truth, we were beneficiaries too. For John modeled in that little discussion circle in his tiny Mews apartment, and in his masterly summings up at the end of each evening, how to grapple with the Bible and the modern world—and how to put them together. The same was true in the discussion groups that John convened for the landmark series of sermons that later became the groundbreaking book *Issues Facing Christians Today*, now in its fourth edition. It was a mark of his care and scholarship that those sermons should be informed not only by a remarkable depth of reading in the subjects he tackled but by drawing in people who knew something of the issues at first hand to earth and authenticate John's own analysis.

In 1989 I accepted an invitation to join Christian Debate, another small group John ran in his apartment, this time for rather more senior figures like Fred Catherwood, John Taylor, Duncan Vere, Michael Alison and Michael Schluter. Again, papers were read, books discussed, contemporary and theological themes explored, and authors occasionally interrogated in person. It was a mark of the personal regard in which John was held that major theologians like N. T. (Tom) Wright were prepared to accept invitations to be grilled (very politely) on their works. I recall a memorable evening with Tom Wright in early 2001 when we debated themes from his recently published book *The Challenge of Jesus*. These evenings, less frequent and with perhaps a shade more gravitas than the reading group, were essentially about exactly the same thing—developing our Christian minds. This passion of John's was, of course, reflected in so much of his preaching and later given institutional manifestation in the London Institute for Contemporary Christianity, which he founded and to which he remained so committed.

But it would be misleading to leave the impression that all this amounted merely to arid intellectualism in John. On the contrary, he combined all this study and analysis with unmistakable emotion and passion. He liked to quote Rabbi Saunders from Chaim Potok's *The Chosen* (a reading group hit!)—"a mind without a heart is nothing." Likewise (quoting Handley Moule), John abhorred in equal measure "undevotional theology" (mind without heart) and "untheological devotion" (heart without mind).

The other major debt I owe John is linked to vocation. I recall early on in my legal career going to see him to discuss the possibility of leaving the bar, at which I was just beginning to practice, to explore possibilities of ordination. He was gracious but firm in discouraging me from that route. "We need Christian lawyers," he said. The seriousness with which he took so-called secular work was wonderfully affirming. There was no message that such work would be second best, there was no arena in which God's people were not needed, where they could not serve effectively. I know he reflected a lot on the "salt and light" metaphors of Matthew 5. He liked to stress the radical difference that Christlikeness demanded. To that distinctiveness, however, there needed to be added permeation of non-Christian society. Salt did no good if it stayed in the saltshaker. Finally, he was powerfully persuaded of the capacity of Christians to change society. Salt hinders bacterial decay. Light dispels darkness. This was not a call to create a perfect society—John knew that was an impossible brief—but it was a call to be incarnated in society, to be "in it but not of it," to improve it. That teaching, which I heard and read in many different strands from John, has proved vocationally steadying for me in what is by now nearly thirty-five years as a barrister and judge.

There have been many other lessons I have learned from this remarkable man. Not least, as a lawyer I covet his drafting skill, his clarity of expression orally and in writing, his linguistic and grammatical precision. I have seen for myself the care with which he prepares for meetings, the strategic thinking with which he plans ahead, his self-discipline, his humility, his concern for others and for the ministry of All Souls Church. In later years membership of his little support group AGE was a great privilege. It was not at all easy for John to accept reduced travel and ministry opportunities, and in time the physical limitations of old age. But even in the hard times, the twinkle in his eye and the mischievous aside were rarely far away.

I recently came upon a letter that John had written to me in mid-1994. It is a letter which nicely sums up the private and the public man. He wrote from his beloved The Hookses in Wales (why was he not off duty?). He anticipated my forthcoming fortieth birthday (how did he know?), bringing his "congratulations or commiserations as you plunge into middle age!" He moved on to

address an All Souls' issue he had earlier raised with me as churchwarden (why did he care so much?) and then he concluded (with
typical humility),

> I hope to finish the page proofs of *Romans* [his superb BST
> commentary] today [all 432 pages of them!]. I confess I am
> not too displeased with some of the exposition; other parts
> seem to me turgid and obfuscatory! I wish I'd taken more
> time to clarify and improve them. Too late now, alas!

This was typical John! Pastoral, humorous, businesslike, disciplined, frighteningly productive—all at the same time. And all of
it compressed on two sides of paper in the neat, unmistakable
handwriting in which, for over sixty years, he recorded and com-
municated the Spirit-inspired thoughts and ideas which made him
a giant of the church of the twentieth century and a wonderful
inspiration to so many of us.

INTERNATIONAL
INFLUENCE

14

REACHING OUT TO TOUCH
THE ENDS OF THE EARTH FOR GOD

MARCUS LOANE

Sir Marcus Loane, after serving as principal of Moore Theological College, was the Anglican archbishop of Sydney from 1966 to 1982 and primate of Australia from 1978 to 1982. He was awarded the KBE (Knight Commander of the Order of the British Empire) in 1976. He and his wife, Patricia, celebrated their seventieth wedding anniversary in 2007. Sir Marcus died in 2009 at the age of ninety-seven.

John Stott first came to Sydney in June 1958 to conduct a mission for the Sydney University Evangelical Union. Ten crowded days followed, during which it seemed as though his voice was never silent, until he lost it almost completely not long before the final meeting in the Great Hall. But God gave him strength to see it through to the end. During this most memorable mission, he stayed in our home at Moore College and won a lasting place in the hearts of our children. News of his father's death reached him only two hours before he was due to speak. But in spite of his own sadness, he rose to the occasion.

John returned many times to Sydney and was ever welcome in our home for every visit. His fame in Australia was spreading. Once he came only for four full days, en route to New Zealand. I met him at the airport on Anzac Day, Friday, April 25, at 6 a.m. Very few people were around at that early hour, but we were interrupted by two young women journalists who pleaded for a brief interview with him, to which he agreed. One of them eventually closed her notebook and said how glad she was to have met him, as she had read a number of his books. The next day I drove him to Mount Wilson in the Blue Mountains, with its dense rainforest, rich in bird life. After a picnic lunch, we followed a narrow track that emerged at length in a little clearing at the back of a cottage. A girl was standing at the old gate leading to the bush. I recognized her as the daughter of one of our headmasters. So I went over to speak to her, while John pursued a woodpecker. Almost at once, another girl appeared whom I did not know. "Oh," she exclaimed, "is that John Stott? Could I meet him?" Now in those days John was said to have been more willing to run a mile than to meet a girl. But he came over and spoke to her. She told him that she had often listened to tapes of his sermons. So I thought to myself, *How remarkable! Within forty-eight hours of arrival in Sydney, having hardly met anyone outside our family, John has encountered two people who have either read his books or listened to his taped sermons.*

Everyone knew how eagerly John would seize every leisure moment for birdwatching. He once rebuked me for what he described as my deficiency in the science of ornithology (or as he sometimes called it, "ornitheology"). I could only ask him in reply if he had ever considered how St John the Divine had planted an ornithological allusion in the heart of the book of Revelation. What was that? The cry of the wild eagle in the gathering storm: "Woe! Woe! Woe!" (Revelation 8:13). John was quite startled!

No visitor from overseas was ever more welcome in our home

or among evangelical clergy and congregations in Sydney. We learned to know how his life was shaped by his discipline and devotion of the highest order. Meticulous preparation meant that he was never at a loss for a word in preaching. His clear and beautiful voice, his flawless diction, his persuasive logic and appeal all marked him out as one in a thousand. I am bound to say again what I have often said before: John Stott was for our generation all that Charles Simeon had been for his generation. Stott at All Souls in London, like Simeon at Holy Trinity at Cambridge—each for more than fifty years, reaching out to touch the ends of the earth for God.

THE PROLIFIC AUTHOR
AND HIS MIDWIFE

FRANK ENTWISTLE

Frank Entwistle, formerly chief executive of IVP (UK), worked closely with John Stott for almost thirty years on John Stott's own books and on the series The Bible Speaks Today. Now retired and living in North Devon, he serves as chairman of John Stott's Literary Executors.

It has been my great privilege to be John Stott's midwife. Writing a book and giving birth have a lot in common. A book is an intensely personal product of an author's thought and experience. It usually has a long gestation before it is "born," and then the author is very concerned about how people will receive it. Throughout the process the publisher is there to help and support, but of course the book is not his but the author's. So how did I come to be John's literary midwife?

I first heard John speak in 1956, when he came to lead the Christian Union mission at Durham University, where I was a first-year undergraduate. Durham had a fine theology faculty and two Anglican theological colleges. The scrutiny that such a setting engendered was especially intense that year. There had recently been a long "fundamentalism" correspondence in *The Times*, provoked by Billy Graham's Cambridge mission the previous year. This led to an outspoken attack on "fundamentalists" and an alternative series of lectures in the university by Michael Ramsey, then bishop of Durham. As a first-year theological student I was deeply impressed by the way John conducted himself in such a charged atmosphere, by his graciousness and by the clarity of his expositions of biblical Christianity. These impressions were reinforced at his second Durham mission in 1959.

After these early opportunities to hear John, my acquaintance with him was no more than that of any other evangelical clergyman of my generation. I was delighted to listen to him at conferences or at Keswick and grateful for his books and leadership, especially at the Keele Congress in 1967. But I doubt that he knew who I was; my Lancashire grammar-school background was very different from his, and it was a long time before I even set foot in All Souls!

So it was a daunting prospect when, having joined the IVP staff in 1973, I was asked to work with John on the Bible Speaks Today series. I confess that I held him in some awe! It was with trepidation that I ascended for the first time the little staircase leading to his study. I was grateful for his concern to put me at my ease, his readiness to welcome me into the large company of his friends and even to seek my opinion. Twenty-three years later, John, ever the planner, decided to set up a group of literary executors and honored me by asking me to be their chairman.

The "baby" analogy only becomes mildly ridiculous when we consider the size of John's literary family. Timothy Dudley-Smith, while working on the two-volume biography, compiled a reference book: *John Stott: A Comprehensive Bibliography*.[1] This covered the years 1939-1994 and extended to 156 pages, of which no less than fifty-six are occupied by an alphabetical list of the titles of John's published writings, including interviews, reviews and sermon notes as well as articles and books, booklets and pamphlets.

Nor do I need to say much about the value of his offspring. As his literary midwife I saw many of his books come to birth over a period of nearly thirty years. Throughout this time there was no doubt that John was one of the world's leading evangelical authors. His new books were eagerly awaited, assiduously collected and translated into many languages. Countless pastors and preachers around the world are delighted to have them on their shelves as a lifetime resource. As his publisher, it was a happy year when I could go to a major international book fair with a new book from John Stott in my bag.

So what was it like to be his literary midwife? What was he like to work with, as an author and editor? Let's think about the different stages of bringing a book to birth—and beyond.

A baby begins at conception, and a book begins with an idea. The idea often comes from the author, sometimes from the publisher. If it comes from the publisher, the author must make it his own, must really want to write the book. Most of John's books originated in his own thinking about what was needed and what he wanted to do. John had a very strong strategic vision. Books were written and published because he believed that they were needed, and he hoped to be able to make a contribution. Yet he was certainly open to suggestions. *The Cross of Christ*, one of his most important books, originated in a suggestion from IVP.

With great anticipation I would receive a book proposal from John, usually a careful outline of several pages. From this, I would have a clear idea of what the book would cover and the way he was proposing to handle the subject. This is perhaps the equivalent of the scans that often take place in the early stages of pregnancy. The parents will be anxious to know that all is well with their new child. Similarly, John would be eager to know what we thought of his proposal and keen to receive our comments. It was seldom that we had anything but praise for the content, though we might venture to express concern about the likely length of the book. Often, he would win such arguments, and in any case he probably guessed (rightly) that we would be able to sell a major book by him, regardless of length.

In the case of John's books, gestation often lasted longer than the biological nine months! He was, of course, very privileged in the facilities that enabled him to write. Several times a year he would go off to The Hookses and nothing was allowed to keep him from those study and writing periods. If I phoned Frances Whitehead to ask about John's availability for a book launch or some other important event, the fact that he would be at The Hookses, or on his way there, on the date in question was enough to guarantee his nonavailability. In this, Frances was only expressing John's own iron discipline.

Even then he would have to juggle claims on his time. Quite often he would report, on his return to London, that he had not made the progress on his IVP book that he had hoped for, because of the need to prepare a course of Bible readings or lectures, or to work on another book.

The gestation of John's books was not to be hurried. Indeed, much of the pressure arose from his own high standards. He was always concerned to do justice to other influential books, especially those that he felt were mistaken. No doubt his study assistants helped greatly in sifting material, but John would grapple with the issues himself until he was satisfied that he had understood all important points of view and come to his own conclusions. Even then he often had misgivings about what he had written on a particular topic, and he would be anxious to know what we and our advisers made of his work.

Eventually the book was done. He wrote all his texts by hand, and they were then beautifully typed by Frances Whitehead. Now the baby could be shown; well, at least the baby in the womb could be examined by the midwife!

The quality of John's writing meant that he was actually very easy to publish. Many authors, especially new authors, need a lot of help in organizing their material or in communicating it. Not so John Stott! It was with joy that our editors received his manuscripts, impeccably typed, as I have said, and needing very little editorial attention. It was our custom, with every book that we were likely to publish, to seek the comments of one or more specialists in the field. John gracefully submitted to this process, wanted to know who those readers were and would then acknowledge their help in his preface.

Then comes the process that probably causes authors most frustration. After the manuscript is received, publishers have several months of work to do before the literary infant can be launched on the world. In the earlier years of our collaboration, much of this was due to the demands of manual copyediting, retyping by typesetters and at least two stages of proofs. Now electronics have speeded up those processes; instead the time is needed for pre-publication marketing and selling of the book around the world, a consequence of the globalization of English-language publishing. Any intelligent author realizes that his or hers is not the only book in the publishing house. Indeed, sometimes they suspect that theirs is at the bottom of a large pile! Of course, John's books were always going to feature prominently in our publishing plans, and he knew that. So there was plenty of pressure to keep the publisher up to the mark.

At last the day of publication would come. John was always ready to cooperate as much as he was able in the launching and promotion of his books. Indeed, he would come if he could to the launch of volumes by other contributors to the Bible Speaks Today series, which was particularly close to his heart (for years he was the editor of the New Testament series). His books often contributed to some current intellectual debate, so he was eager to see reviews and was grateful when his books were taken seriously. And he shared our frustration when they were ignored in the review pages of important periodicals. Of course, it has been a great encouragement to him that so many of his literary offspring have gone on to have a long life and have made a lasting and powerful contribution to the Christian cause worldwide.

John's keen strategic sense can be seen in many aspects of his literary activity. A participant in the British Inter-Varsity movement from his own student days, he recognized a synergy with IVP and made us his primary publisher. Yet he gave some important books to other publishing houses so as to widen his impact. His commitment to the Bible Speaks Today series owed much to his desire to put resources for preaching into the hands of pastors and preachers around the world. He was anxious to include in that series books by authors from Asia and Africa, and it was only after many efforts and disappointments that we had to recognize that those whom we wanted to write were just too busy to do so. In more recent years the series called Global Christian Library (in the United States, Christian Doctrine in Global Perspective), another Stott brainchild, expressed the same desire to provide biblical Christian thinking and teaching by authors from all over the Majority World.

John's longstanding interest in color photography, especially of birds, made him receptive to the suggestion that some of his popular writings might be published with full color illustrations. Following a proposal from Dr. Tim Dowley, *Favorite Psalms* was published in 1988, the first of a number of such volumes. A particular joy to John was *The Birds Our Teachers*,[2] described on the cover as "Biblical lessons from a lifelong birdwatcher" and containing more than 150 photographs by the author. Those who want to know John as a person should read this book! However, Tim Dowley has reminded me that John turned down a suggestion from across the

Atlantic for a pop-up book of birds!

We are all enormously grateful to God for John Stott's literary offspring, the fruit of a lifetime's arduous parenting, and for their influence for Christ and the gospel. The many Christian publishers around the world who have assisted in their birth are deeply thankful, as I am, for that privilege.

A DOUBLE PORTION OF
LANGUAGE SKILLS

KEITH HUNT AND GLADYS HUNT

*Keith Hunt and Gladys Hunt were hosts to John Stott during his
first visit to the United States and Canada in 1956 at the invitation of InterVarsity Christian Fellowship. John Stott returned to
the United States at Keith's invitation many times during the
following decades to speak to student groups and to share some
holidays together. The Hunts coauthored the history of IVCF,
For Christ and the University* (IVP, 1991). *Gladys Hunt, who
wrote many other books, died in July 2010.*

When the Lord God made human beings word partners with
himself, he seemed to give a double portion of language skills to
John Stott. John has used this gift not to entertain or seem erudite,
but to enlighten, using language to enrich spiritual lives. Yet it
was more than the right word choice that made conversations
with John delightful and substantive; it was his disciplined thinking that produced such clarity of thought and keen observations
that one would think, *How is it that I didn't see that before?*

Probably no one has done more to help us love God's Word than
John. We are indebted to him for all the windows into truth that

he has opened for us. When we read his books we hear his voice, his intonations and emphasis. At a student conference we had arranged for university students at Ann Arbor, Michigan, in the mid-1970s, John did the initial expositions on the Sermon on the Mount that later became a full book in the Bible Speaks Today series: *Christian Counter Culture*.[1] Five teaching sessions, each lasting forty-five minutes, held students in thoughtful wonder as Stott illumined the text. We turned to each other when he finished a session to lament with others, "Oh, he's finished already." Few of us had ever heard the Bible taught so clearly.

John Stott's profound input in the American student world also ministered to us personally, because our friendship deepened during many encounters over those years. Only God knows what this faithful servant has meant to the students around the world through his Bible teaching in the member movements of the International Fellowship of Evangelical Students (IFES). Today we meet people who still remember whole outlines from messages he gave as the main Bible expositor at InterVarsity Christian Fellowship's (IVCF's) Urbana Student Missions Convention, so powerful was their impact. At six of these major triennial student missions conventions (1964-1979), John spoke from the Scriptures each morning to thousands of students. "The Word of God rang out" through the words he used.

His use of language is an integral part of who John Stott is. But it is not confined to his preaching and teaching. One of our favorite memories of his use of words, his focus and observations, came in quite another setting. In 1981 we spent a month's holiday with him in Alaska, birdwatching and exploring this last frontier area. During the third week, we traveled by station wagon far north toward the Arctic Circle until the road ended at the Yukon River. In what seemed like the middle of nowhere we stopped, looking for the accommodation we had booked—a rustic one-room cabin in the woods, maintained by the Bureau of Land Management, for two dollars a night. John was effusively apologetic to the young "squatter" who had to move out when we arrived. (A bear had torn up his tent while he had been panning for gold, so he had moved in for cover while waiting the arrival of a new tent.) A stack of mattresses on a single cot, a small table stained with candle wax, sooty windows and a dirty floor greeted us. John took a quick look and queried, "How many nights did you book this for?" Only two. We set to work to polish the place up a bit and crashed for the night. We couldn't beat the price.

The next morning looked much brighter, with a clear blue sky and birds flitting about the picnic table outside the door. The sun was warm, and life looked quite hopeful with a fire cooking bacon, eggs and fried bread, and a cup of hot coffee. Then John spotted a rare hawk owl, a first for him. It was going to be a good day! We took a day trip to look for migrating caribou and to find the town of Circle. The caribou eluded us, but we did find gold miners coming off the Yukon at Circle with stories to tell.

Later that night, returning after dark to our cabin, we sat around the small table by the light of candles and a lantern to talk about the day. We suggested that John read to us from the travel diary he was keeping. It was a perfect setting for hearing him give us his record of our adventure. It was mesmerizing. It was riveting. We saw our travels with fresh eyes. It was descriptive, full of observations (he had watched the drama of a goshawk with a rabbit in its claws), full of information, full of movement—it was alive. And furthermore, it was publishable just as he read it to us! Listening to him read was one of those "Wow!" moments. Our diary, full of half-sentences and half-information, was fit only for the trash heap by comparison. Who could not love this fellow traveler in his wrinkled shirt and jacket, glasses on the end of his nose, with a battered hat on his head, using the same well-chosen words in the candlelight to enrich our memories of this journey as he used in Bible exposition.

John's life with God was tangible when we were with him. But there was much more to his personality than that kind of "sainthood." He enjoyed companionship. John always did the washing-up after our meals together. He would guffaw at the quintessentially British P. G. Wodehouse stories of the blundering Bertie Wooster and his personal gentleman Jeeves. John loved little children, and they found him very easy to relate to. He enjoyed a good movie, liked Woody Allen, relished a good concert, loved walking the streets of London and was very fond of chocolate (in disciplined amounts with a good cup of coffee!). We once gave him a button that said, "Eleven out of ten people love chocolate." Somebody else teased his ecological passion with a fridge sticker saying, "Save the earth: it's the only planet with chocolate."

He did not suffer fools gladly, but he was kind beyond necessity to others who needed encouragement. When we were on St. Paul Island of the Pribilof Islands in Alaska, we went with him to pay a fellow clergy visit to two unusual men who were trying to minister to the Aleut community on this desolate setting in the Bering Sea. One was a Russian Orthodox priest (who had replaced his father as the island priest by attending a two-week course that told him "how to do it"). It appeared that he had little, if any, understanding of the gospel. It was heartwarming to see the gracious dignity John showed this man. The other man and his wife were a couple of adventurers who had built a small Protestant church on the edge of town, hoping people would come. They were lonely people, isolated by their unaccepted religious beliefs. The husband talked mostly about trapping blue fox, and the wife took pleasure in showing John, the Englishman, the members of the royal family she had crafted out of bottles found washed up on the beach each spring. It was a moment of abounding grace when she let in the cat carrying his bird kill and it turned out to be a water pipit! We laughed all the way back to our lodgings over her words, "Naughty, Tommy!" when she saw by contrast how much the death of a water pipit had mattered to John.

No words of ours can adequately convey what this friend has meant to us and how he has influenced our whole family. It's enough to say that we know God better because of knowing John Stott. I doubt he would want us to say more than that.

Growing up

With Bash in the early 1940s

John Stott with David Gitari, 1962

In Australia with Marcus Loane and Jack Dain

John with Martyn Lloyd-Jones at the Second National Assembly of Evangelicals, 1966

Ted Schroder (with John) at John's fiftieth birthday party in the Waldegrave Hall, All Souls, London, 1971

John with Michael Baughen in the run-up to the massive rebuilding project at All Souls in 1974

With the Duchess of Kent and Noel Tredinnick at the Organ Club Golden Jubilee Celebrations at the Royal Festival Hall, London, 1976

With Billy Graham at Sydney Crusade, 1979

"Who is John Stott anyway?" Mark Labberton with John

With Samuel Escobar in Quito, Ecuador, 1985

With Henri Blocher, Andrew Kirk and Peter Kuzmič during the first session of LICC in 1982

*With Richard Bewes,
Weymouth Street, London, 1986
(Photo: Kieran Dodds)*

*"The 'baby' that brought me [Frank] most joy." John with
Frank Entwistle at the launch of* The Cross of Christ *in 1986
(Photo: Keith Ellis Collection)*

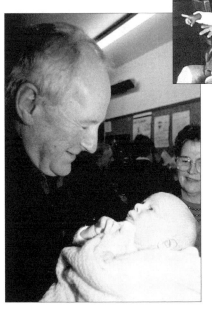

"Look, it's over there."
John, the lover of children

Peter Cranston's baptism
(Photo: Rosemary Cranston)

Table football with Jon and Andy Cranston, 1987
(Photo: Rosemary Cranston)

Another book signing

With Peter Harris on a birding trip to Spain and Morocco in 1989

With Toby Howarth at The Hookses in 1987

Ferry to Whittier, Alaska, with (l to r) Keith and Gladys Hunt, James Houston (one of the founders of Regent College, Vancouver), John, and Rita Houston, August 1981

John on St. Paul Island (Pribilof Islands), Alaska, 1981 (Photo: Keith Hunt)

Just like Lawrence of Arabia! Wearing a keffiyeh to ward off mosquitoes, Michigan, 1975 (Photo: Mark Hunt)

Salmon fishing in Brooks River, Alaska, 1981 (Photo: Keith Hunt)

Astride a giant tortoise in the Galapagos Islands (Photo: René Padilla)

With his Bible at Cedar Campus 1978 (Photo: Mark Hunt)

A bird in the hand—holding a Manx shearwater (Photo: David Cranston)

With Billy Graham and David Jones on the day before the St. Louis Crusade in 1999

John (third from left) and Samuel Escobar (fifth from left), Chris Wright (sixth from left) and pastors at the first Langham Preaching Seminar in Peru in 2001

Kneeling before a cockerel for the perfect shot! (Photo: David Cranston)

With Corey Widmer in Uganda in 2000

With Matthew Smith, John Smith and Myra Chave-Jones at the back door of The Hookses

In his study at The Hookses (Photo: David Cranston)

John with Frances Whitehead at The Hookses, September 2007

Relaxing by fireside at The Hookses (Photo: David Cranston)

In search of another perfect photo opportunity

Enjoying Saki and chocolates—the perfect combination

Later years. On his way to St. Bride's Church with Neil Woodward and Chris Jones
(Photo: David Cranston)

In his study with
Frances Whitehead
(Photo: Kieran Dodds)

At the door of
12 Weymouth Street
(Photo: Kieran Dodds)

17

Mentor and Model
to Emerging Younger Leaders

AJITH FERNANDO

*Ajith Fernando has been national director of Youth for Christ in
Sri Lanka since 1976. He also has an international Bible teaching ministry, including the Lausanne Movement and Urbana
Student Missions Conventions, and has written many books.
His parents were friends of John Stott, and reading Stott's Bible
expositions from his father's library gave Ajith a taste for biblical expository preaching.*

I would find it hard to say which of two things about John Stott
has influenced me more: his model preaching, teaching and writing, or his model lifestyle of godly humility. I was greatly inspired
by his example in both areas when I was a younger leader whom
he mentored and encouraged, along with countless others of my
generation.

My initial contact with John was through his books. I had a
sense that I was going to be a minister from the time I was about
fourteen years old. My father was an evangelical lay leader who
had a large library. Among his books were the compendia of talks

given at the Urbana Student Missions Conventions in the United States and the Keswick Convention. These introduced me to the Bible expositions of John Stott and others, and gave me a passion for Bible exposition during my teenage years. While I was a university student, I read Stott's book *The Preacher's Portrait*. I regard this as one of the most influential books in my life because it helped me to develop convictions and ambitions about Christian ministry that still shape my life. These books led me to the conviction that expounding a Bible passage should be the primary method of Christian preaching. Later, after reading Stott's *I Believe in Preaching*, I began to view topical preaching also as coming under the category of expository preaching—provided the points come directly from Scripture.

My own style of preaching was subsequently also influenced by Methodist preachers like W. E. Sangster and E. Stanley Jones, and by the Indian evangelist Sadhu Sunder Singh, especially by their use of illustrations and their style of application. But the primary influence remained the expository preaching of John Stott. He taught me that all preaching is the result of biblical exegesis. You can imagine the personal thrill with which I responded to an invitation to be the Bible expositor at the Urbana Student Missions Convention in 1987 (and since on three other occasions). It was a joy to do what my mentor had done many times before. I had a similar thrill when I followed his three expositions on Romans 1–5 with two expositions on Romans 6–8 at the Lausanne II Congress in Manila in 1989.

I first met John when I was a student at Fuller Theological Seminary in the mid-1970s, where he spent a day preaching and speaking with the students. After a question-and-answer session, he came up to me. "Do I know you, brother?" he asked. "No," I said, "but you know my parents." He immediately knew who I was and gave me a hug. After that, I walked a few feet above ground level for a couple of days! Later he would send me complimentary copies of his books and sign them with the words, "With esteem and affection, Uncle John." What esteem could this giant have for a young unknown youth worker? And what qualifications did I have for him to call himself "Uncle John" when writing to me? These gifts of books introduced me to another aspect of Stott's great contribution to the church—his efforts to support and enable younger leaders to achieve their fullest potential.

I was included in the Lausanne Committee for World Evangelization as a "younger member," and my first meeting as a member was in 1980 at the Lausanne Consultation in Pattaya, Thailand. There some of the representatives of the younger radical wing of the evangelical community raised their voices and pushed for a stronger emphasis on justice and social responsibility within the Lausanne Movement, in faithfulness to the Lausanne Covenant of 1974. My experience and battles within a mainline denomination caused me to be alarmed at some of the things I was hearing. I even pointed out the need for caution in the way we responded to this challenge. But Stott spoke up after I did and appealed to the committee to listen to these younger leaders. He pointed out that their concerns were genuine and highlighted some blind spots within the evangelical movement. This was a great help to me as I faced these challenges in my ministry. I learned to do all I could to help give expression to these voices while at the same time attempting to act as a watchdog for evangelism, which could so easily be neglected as we open ourselves to other essential aspects of the mission of the church. Like Barnabas, Stott had used his moral authority and esteem as an acknowledged leader to sponsor and encourage younger creative thinkers.

In 1978 I attended the Lausanne-sponsored Asian Leadership Conference on Evangelism (ALCOE) in Singapore, where Stott was the Bible expositor. It was two years after I had returned to Sri Lanka, following my theological studies in the United States, to serve with Youth for Christ. When John saw me, after his customary hug, he proceeded to ask me if I was giving time to study. This was, and still is, one of the biggest challenges that I face, and the fact that this was the first thing he asked me showed me how important it is. That encounter encouraged me to persevere in squeezing in time for study in the three decades that followed. The idea of "squeezing in time" also came to me from John when he visited Fuller Seminary during my student days. Someone asked him, "How do you find time to study?" He answered that in an earlier era ministers could spend weekday mornings studying, but that this was not practical in today's world. So we must always be ready to study at any time and use every possible opportunity to do so. As a result of this advice I got into the habit of taking books everywhere I went and taking notes as I read—at bus stands, banks, government departments, and in trains, planes, airports and police stations. All of these were places I needed to visit often, as our staff and volunteers were often arrested because of the unrest in Sri Lanka. Sometimes people see me taking notes as I read and ask me if I am studying for an exam!

One book I read by "squeezing in time" in that way was what I regard as the most enriching doctrinal book I have ever read: *The Cross of Christ*. I took it with me wherever I went for about four months—making copious notes in the margins, composing a detailed table of contents at the front and compiling my own index at the back. Once I was traveling back by bus from a camp in the mountains. I read it at the bus stand while I waited for the bus and then I read in the bus when it stopped to drop and pick up passengers. It was about a six-hour journey, and I had to stand because the bus was full. When the bus was moving I kept the book on a rack above the seats. Suddenly someone said that a book had fallen out of the bus through the window. I knew it was my book and I took my bag and got out of the bus to go in search of it.

Some people walking along the road informed me that someone in a bus coming in the opposite direction had seen the book fall

out, had stopped their bus, picked it up and continued their journey. As I was talking with these people by the roadside, a police
jeep came along. They asked what had happened and, when I explained the situation, they let me get into the jeep and we gave
chase to the bus! We finally caught up with it, as it had stopped in
the next town. I gratefully took possession of the book and proceeded on my journey. This was a book I could not afford to lose
and replace with a new copy, because I had already made so many
notes in it.

Stott's *The Cross of Christ* is an example of another thing that
made him a mentor to many of us younger Christian workers.
From his pen came definitive treatments of many key doctrinal
and ethical issues facing the church. John Stott's books were bibli-
cally astute, theologically informed and fully aware of the context
of the society we live in. In this category I would also include his
Christian Mission in the Modern World, I Believe in Preaching and
Issues Facing Christians Today. These books were the result of what
Stott called "double listening," devoting one's energy to understanding both God's Word and God's world. During a question-
and-answer time at the ALCOE Conference in 1978, someone
asked Stott what were the key requirements for effective contextu-
alization. He answered that the first requirement is that we must
know the Bible. Only then did he go on to talk about other requirements. I, in turn, determined that everything we do in our
ministry with youth must spring from a solid biblical theology.
John Stott's definitive treatments not only gave us vital information on key issues but also a model of how we should approach all
issues in ministry from a thorough biblical foundation.

I have tried to adapt Stott's biblical approach to all the topical
books I have written. I did so even when I disagreed with him. I
completed my book *Crucial Questions About Hell* shortly after Stott
had stated that he was open to the possibility (as a biblical view-
point) of the ultimate annihilation of the finally unrepentant, as

opposed to their eternal conscious torment. This was published in *Essentials: A Liberal-Evangelical Dialogue*, which he coauthored as a series of conversations with liberal theologian David Edwards. I came to the painful realization that I was going to have to oppose my hero! I mentioned his name only in the endnotes, but I sought to respond to the points he made in that book. After completing the chapter and before sending the book to the publisher, I sent it to John. He wrote back saying that both he and I needed to do some more careful study of the Bible.

Another huge impact that John Stott had on me was through his simple and humble lifestyle. I was on the planning team for the Lausanne Younger Leaders' Conference, Singapore, in 1987. There was no doubt that the hero of this conference was John Stott. But he distinguished himself by *not* speaking at it. He did give one short message, but he was there for the whole conference—that is, for over a week—just so that he could be an encouragement to the younger leaders. He devoted every spare moment to personal appointments with the delegates. It was clear that behind the greatness of this man as a communicator of Christian truth was a love for people and a commitment to personal ministry.

John Stott's concern for younger leaders is well represented by the correspondence he continued to have with many of us. My friend Peter Kuzmič, from Croatia, tells how he once went to an airport chapel to pray. In the front of the chapel he could see the head of an older man and scores of papers that he seemed to be arranging according to different categories. Upon closer observation he discovered that it was John arranging a huge pile of letters. I used to be amazed that he had time to write to me. Later I realized that if I am to have an international ministry, I must also have a ministry of international intercession and correspondence. We influence people in our travels, and we need to pray for them and encourage them through correspondence.

I had one unforgettable opportunity to visit John Stott in his little flat. I was thrilled to note the simplicity of the place and to see the kneeler where he prayed. But what thrilled me most was a question he asked me: "How is Jeyaraj?" Jeyaraj was a colleague who had been arrested on suspicion of being a terrorist and who had spent fifteen months in prison before being released without any charges being made against him. I had asked for prayer for him in my semi-annual prayer letter. And I found that not only did John remember Jeyaraj's name, he also remembered to pray for him.

In contrast to John Stott's simple humility, today's model of the lifestyle of the successful Christian leader has taken in many features from a model prevalent in society. In Asia this is further enhanced by the model of the religious gurus who live on a different plane than the people and are venerated with an adoration one would give a god-man. These leaders usually travel with a large entourage, stay in luxury hotels, own big cars and houses, and have a strong public relations machine which helps push forward their reputation. There is a strong temptation to imagine that such things are indicators of a significant ministry. All vocational Christian workers want to do something significant for God. But John showed us that it is possible to have a huge influence without these trappings of worldly success. So when *Time* magazine included John in a list of the hundred most influential people in the world, and when the *New York Times* wrote of his huge impact on the Christian church, we felt that it was an affirmation of some of the difficult vocational and lifestyle decisions we had made, following his example in the way of simplicity.

As for me, his example has helped me to remain in Sri Lanka, serving Youth for Christ for the past thirty-four years. And now, as I approach the prospect of stepping down from leadership, his example of remaining under the umbrella of All Souls Church, Langham Place, spurs me to seek a way I can remain accountable to Youth for Christ, even after stepping down from the national directorship. His example also helped me decide to live on a Sri Lankan salary and to divert my royalties and honoraria to Youth for Christ for literature and education projects. I have felt that doing this has given me the freedom to minister worldwide without any sense of guilt or secrecy, knowing that everything I do in ministry is done as a worker of Youth for Christ.

18

On the Road with John Stott

SAMUEL ESCOBAR

Samuel Escobar, from Peru, has a lifetime association with the International Fellowship of Evangelical Students (IFES), exercising years of leadership in Latin America and Canada, and speaking many times at the Urbana Student Missions Convention. He worked closely with John Stott at the 1974 Lausanne Congress. He is a missiologist, with books in Spanish and English, and taught at Eastern Baptist Theological Seminary, Pennsylvania. He now lives in Valencia, Spain, with his wife, Lilly, where he is involved in theological education.

What a privilege it has been from time to time in the last fifty years to walk alongside John Stott in a variety of places and situations around the world.

It all started in March 1959 when Bob Young, a staff member of IFES, gave me a copy of John Stott's recently published *Basic Christianity*. We were traveling through Ecuador, en route from Peru to Colombia, trying to start student groups for evangelism and leadership training. The road from Quito to Tulcán was not paved and it was bumpy, but I could not put the book away. I devoured this clear and convincing presentation of the Christian faith from an evangelical perspective. It became one of the first books that IFES published in Spanish.

Later that year, in July, I met John Stott personally when I was among a group of student workers who had attended the General Committee of IFES in Paris. We were hosted by the British IVF for a ten-day training program with a select group of British evangelical scholars. They arranged a visit to Cambridge, and John was our guide. I have a clear image of his elegant figure as he walked us through the corridors of Cambridge University and shared the stories of the evangelical student movement (CICCU) in that city. During our walk I was able to talk with him personally. I thanked him effusively as I shared the story of my encounter with *Basic Christianity.*

Next time we walked together was in Berlin, November 1966, during the World Congress of Evangelism, organized by Billy Graham. At the time I was taking doctoral courses at the Complutense University in Madrid, Spain, during an IFES sabbatical after my first seven years of student work in Peru, Brazil and Argentina. Working among university students during the agitated years that followed the Cuban revolution, we could not avoid questions about the social responsibility of Christians and especially of evangelicals. With René Padilla, who had returned from his doctoral studies in Manchester under F. F. Bruce, we tried to articulate an evangelical perspective on social responsibility. René proposed that it should be Christ centered: following the outline of incarnation, crucifixion and resurrection. In Berlin, John gave four Bible lectures about the Great Commission, and I was particularly touched by his exposition of John 20:21 and his emphasis on the incarnation as our model for missionary presence and action. It resonated with what René Padilla and I had been working on for years. As we talked again in Berlin, I was impressed that John would call me by my name. He told me also that since our encounter in Cambridge he had prayed regularly for IFES in Latin America and for René and myself. Since Berlin I have treasured both his lectures and our conversation as formative highlights of my ministry.

Four years later I walked alongside John in the snow, in the cold winter of Urbana, Illinois, during the Urbana Student Missions Convention in December 1970. The convention was marked by the atmosphere of student activism and protest that was the mood of American campuses at that time. In 1969, as a follow-up to the Berlin 1966 congress, we had held the largest ever gathering of Latin American evangelicals in the First Congress of Evangelism (CLADE I) in Bogotá, Colombia. My paper on the social responsibility of the church, which had good quotes from John's exposition in Berlin, had been received with a standing ovation. I had developed the outline on which we had been working with René during the 1960s, and it was evident that evangelicals felt we had answered some of their questions and concerns. At Urbana 1970, John Stott tried to respond to the acute questions of students motivated by speakers such as the pacifist Mennonite Myron Augsburger and black evangelist Tom Skinner. We were aware that it was important to revisit the radical nature of Jesus' teaching and its bearing on the social responsibility of evangelicals. We had to help students not to be simply carried away by the radical activism of the post-May 1968 agitation, but to develop a distinctly evangelical approach to social issues.

At the next student conference, Urbana 1973, our paths crossed again and we spoke about the preparations for the 1974 Lausanne Congress on World Evangelization. Both of us were going to be speakers, and we shared our gratitude to God for the growing awareness about the proclamation of the gospel in obedience to the Great Commission, as well as a renewed attention to the Great Command to love our neighbor and serve human needs. We were aware that it was not easy to get evangelicals to cooperate, but I was touched by John's openness to hear all voices and to respect different positions. In January 1974 John was going to visit Mexico, Peru, Chile and Argentina, and at Urbana he shared with me his sense of expectation about this first visit to Latin America. At the time I was general director of IVCF Canada, and it would later be a joy for me to welcome John in Toronto for an IVCF evening banquet. My wife, Lilly, finally met him there and she was touched by his gracious kindness. "He looks a saint," she said.

Then Lausanne took place in 1974, and John Stott played a significant key role as he chaired the committee that gave final form to the Lausanne Covenant. A small committee was formed to work on the final text of the covenant, including Hudson Armerding, Leighton Ford, John Stott and myself, with J. D. Douglas as a consultant. John chaired it in a masterful way. An initial draft had been circulated to participants, inviting written responses and comments. We spent long hours discussing diverse and sometimes conflicting positions. On this occasion I was not *walking* with John Stott but running alongside him at great speed. With his unique ability to express in clear language the ideas about which we had a consensus, we were able to come to a final rich, clear, readable text that could be understood by the average Christian around the world.

By the time John came for his second trip through Latin America in 1977, ten of his books had been translated into Spanish by three different publishing houses, and his name was already well known and respected. People enjoyed his Bible expositions, which even through translation had the clarity and forcefulness of his pastoral and teaching style. From early June to July 1977 he was the main speaker at pastoral retreats in Mexico, Guatemala, Ecuador and Argentina, attended by hundreds of pastors and leaders. At the end of the pastoral retreat in Córdoba, Argentina, where we were living at the time, Lilly and I had the great joy and honor of hosting him at our home. We treasure the long conversations of those two days, even though he had a cold—a cold he had caught by going out one freezing morning to watch birds on the roof of the convent where the pastoral retreat was held.

In the process of global reflection that followed Lausanne, John played a unique and valuable role. His traveling ministry around the world had sensitized him to the reality of a multicultural church. Evangelicalism itself had different faces in different cultures, and he was a careful hearer and observer, and a respectful interlocutor. His gift for words and clarity was exercised still further as he worked with different teams to give final form to the documents of the post-Lausanne consultations that were organized by the Lausanne Theology and Education Group. In Latin America we appreciated especially the final reports from the consultations on "Gospel and Culture"[1] and "Evangelism and Social Responsibility."[2] It was significant that a man like John Stott, with a high view of the inspiration and authority of Scripture, and in whose ministry Bible exposition was central, would come to acknowledge that a culturally contextual approach was required for the interpretation of God's Word.

In 1983 the World Assembly of IFES was held in England. John Stott invited me to present a series of Bible expositions at the London Institute for Contemporary Christianity. Lilly and I were housed in John's apartment, not far from All Souls Church, and one day we spent an unforgettable evening with him. First, he drove us for a picnic in Hyde Park, at which he acted as a most gracious host for a full English tea on the grass, and then he took us to a concert at the Royal Albert Hall. Lilly said more than once that she thought she was dreaming. We all enjoyed a great conversation about the times when we had been together in different parts of the world. During that period, every year I would receive a gift of fifty pounds from John for buying books. Several other evangelical leaders from other parts of the world benefited also in this way.

In 1985 Stott came to Quito, Ecuador, for the month-long IFES Continental Seminar for senior leaders. Seventy-five students and graduates from sixteen countries attended. During the first week John spoke about the authority of the Bible, and during the second he presented a five-part series about the person of Jesus Christ. He also held a seminar for several hundred pastors on Bible exposition. His book *La Contracultura Cristiana (Christian Counter-Culture)*, an exposition of the Sermon on the Mount, had just been published. The meeting was held in a convent, and the old building had no facilities to provide hot water. At an altitude of about 13,000 feet, the mornings were very cold, and taking a shower was a trial. John laughed about it and said that as a good Englishman he had no problem with it. I walked with him while we talked about my moving to the United States to teach missiology at Eastern Baptist Seminary in Philadelphia, and we both embraced and encouraged Brazilian-born Dieter Brepohl, my successor as associate secretary of IFES for Latin America.

Fifteen years after Lausanne, a follow-up, Lausanne II, was celebrated in Manila in 1989. The conference was held in a Majority World city in which the contrasts between modern technology and architecture stood side by side with dire poverty and evidences of corruption and injustice. Among the younger speakers were Brazilian Valdir Steuernagel and South African Cesar Molebatsi, representatives of a new evangelical generation whose presentations were marked by what came to be known as "the spirit of Lausanne." As we walked together during those days, John and I shared in thanksgiving to God, though we were also aware that there was a long way to go in putting into practice the commitments of the Lausanne Covenant around the world. The new vision was outlined in the Manila Manifesto.

Our most recent walk together was in Lima, Peru, in October 2001, when John came with Chris Wright for a Langham preaching seminar. A selected group of pastors and leaders had arrived from several cities of Peru for an intensive week of Bible expositions and practical workshops. We all watched John, who was by now eighty years old and looking somewhat weak and frail. But when he spoke, it was as if a new energy possessed him, and the clarity, forcefulness and pastoral wealth of his words were again Stott at his best.

One day, after the seminar had ended, we walked together in the district of Miraflores, in Lima. The traffic was intense in the avenue that we were trying to cross. John had Chris on his right and myself on his left as we tried to help him avoid any mishap. Suddenly, in a brief moment in which there was a short interval in the flow of cars, he surprised us by jumping across the two-lane avenue and crossing it in just a few steps. As Chris and I caught up with him, John greeted us with a triumphant smile: "Do not forget," he said, "that I live in London and in that city there are only two kinds of people: the quick and the dead."

As I read and recommend the treasure of John Stott's writings in Spanish, I praise God for his ministry, and my memory frequently goes back with joy to my many walks alongside a servant of God, from whose life and thought I have learned so much.

"Jesus Told Us to Wash One Another's Feet . . . I Can Clean Your Shoes"

RENÉ PADILLA

René Padilla was born in Quito, Ecuador. He established and led International Fellowship of Evangelical Students (IFES) movements throughout Latin America and has been a foremost writer and publisher in the field of integral/holistic mission. He was a significant speaker at the first Lausanne Congress in 1974. He is president emeritus of the Kairos Foundation, Buenos Aires, Argentina, where he lives. He regards his long-time friend John Stott as the person that best embodies for him the Pauline invitation "Be imitators of me, as I am of Christ."

I first met John Stott in England in 1959, shortly after I had joined the staff of the International Fellowship of Evangelical Students. In the following years we saw each other very briefly two or three times, but I was surprised when, in 1964, while doing doctoral studies at the University of Manchester and after a Sunday morning service at All Souls Church, John greeted me by name. Years later I realized that one of John's most wonderful gifts was that of remembering people by name, sometimes years after he had met them.

Twice I had the privilege of traveling with John all the way from Mexico to Argentina for one whole month. The first occasion was in 1974, before Lausanne I, and the second was in 1977, shortly after the Consultation on the Homogeneous Unit Principle. Those two trips gave me the opportunity to know John much more deeply than I ever could have done otherwise.

Those trips were a remarkable combination of Christian ministry and—birdwatching! I still have the binoculars that he bought for me so that I could join him in his birdwatching expeditions. I did enjoy the experience, but I must admit that, despite the fact that he was more than ten years older than me, it was almost always difficult for me to keep up with him. Aside from that, I soon found out that birdwatching for him was far more than just watching birds: it was identifying them by name (and he kept an amazing number of names in his mind!) and also waiting for the birds to be in the right position to be photographed. More than once I decided to dedicate my time to reading while waiting for John to photograph birds. However, I was sold on birdwatching after John and I saw a whole family of condors flying over us near Lima, Peru. A beautiful sight! John celebrated that occasion as my "conversion." But a couple of years later, when he asked me how I was doing with my birdwatching and I told him that I was not practicing it, he called me a "backslider."

John was used by God as a key figure at Lausanne I. I was invited to read a plenary paper at the Congress on the topic "Evangelism and the World." In it, I raised a number of issues that I believed needed to be carefully examined by evangelicals, such as the question of lifestyle, the use of the "homogeneous unit principle" for church growth, and the relationships between gospel and culture, and between evangelism and social responsibility. As a result, I was treated with suspicion and rejected by a large section of the evangelical establishment, especially in the United States. All of these issues, however, found a place in the Lausanne Covenant. Furthermore, I remain deeply grateful to John for making sure that these same issues were taken up at the series of consultations that he organized between 1977 and 1982, as chairman of the Lausanne Theology and Education Group of the Lausanne Movement. To all of them he invited me as one of the main speakers.

The more I got to know John, the more impressed I was by two traits of his Christian character. The first one was the diligence with which he prepared himself every time he had to expound Scripture. During both of our trips we made several stops along the way, and that meant that we could repeat the same messages three or four times as we addressed different audiences. What I noticed was that regardless of how many times he had already preached a given sermon he would still spend considerable time before delivering it again, going over the outline and praying over it. Every presentation of a sermon required the most diligent preparation.

The second trait that really impressed me was his humility. I have never forgotten his demonstration of it in Bariloche, a beautiful Argentine city near the Chilean border. We arrived rather late at night, under pouring rain. In order to get to the room where we were to stay overnight, we had to walk a distance. The path was very muddy, and we got our shoes quite dirty. We were tired, so we went to bed right away. Next day I was woken by a sound. When I opened my eyes, I saw John sitting on his bed—brushing my shoes! "John!" I said, "what are you doing?" "My dear René," he responded, "Jesus told us to wash one another's feet. Today we do not wash feet the way people did in Jesus' day, but I can clean your shoes." Several times I heard John preach on humility; many times I saw him putting it into practice.

Breakfast by Appointment
at the Stottery

DAVID GITARI

David Gitari, after serving as bishop of Mount Kenya East and Kirinyaga from 1975 to 1996, was appointed archbishop of the Anglican Church of Kenya in 1997—a post he held until his retirement in 2002. His ministry has been marked by passionate evangelism and remarkable church growth, zeal for theological education and courageous commitment to the social and political challenge of the gospel. Now living in retirement in Kenya, he is still active in writing, speaking and theological education.

I first met John Stott when he was conducting a mission at the Royal College, Nairobi, Kenya, in 1962. As chairman of the Christian Union I was very much involved in the planning. John Stott came to Nairobi from West Africa with a swollen eyelid. A mosquito in Ghana had bitten him. He told us that the British had found it difficult to colonize West African countries because of mosquitoes and malaria. Despite his swollen eyelid he spoke powerfully and demonstrated that the gospel can be defended intellectually.

I kept in touch with John Stott by correspondence. Then I became a theological student at Tyndale Hall, Bristol, from 1965 until 1966. John invited me to stay at his home in London, which was called the "Stottery." I stayed at the Stottery with fellow Kenyan student George Kinoti, who later became a professor of biology at the University of Nairobi. I was at the Stottery for one full month and to my surprise I met my host only once! John would wake up very early, take his breakfast alone and then do his pastoral duties or lock himself in his study to prepare his sermons or write books. I had to make an appointment to see him over breakfast during that one month. That was an experience I still remember. It was amazing to me, as an African, that I could stay in a friend's house for a whole month and be able to see him only once, and that by appointment! I am sure John knew his priorities and was a good steward of time. That is why he has been able to achieve so much in his lifetime.

The other incident I remember is that I took John by car to visit Lake Naivasha in Kenya in order to birdwatch. When we arrived John hired a boat, and I stayed in one corner of it reading newspapers. John kept on telling me to look at this or that kingfisher and other birds, but I was totally uninterested. I could not believe how anybody could spend so much time watching birds, and John could not believe how anybody could spend so much time reading newspapers when there were birds to be watched! However, years later John converted me to love birds, though not with quite the same enthusiasm as himself. Since my retirement in 2002, I have been keeping birds such as ducks, geese, doves and peacocks.

John Stott has been my mentor. I have read his books, especially Bible expositions, and have often quoted him in my sermons.

He also had a very good sense of humor. When he came to conduct a retreat for bishops and clergy in Limuru in 1998, I remember him telling us a story of a parish priest who always drank a glass of milk at the pulpit before he started preaching. One Sunday some naughty choirboys removed some of the milk from the glass and filled it up with whisky. So, when the priest went to the pulpit he tasted his glass of milk, hesitated a bit, licked his lips and sipped a little more, and then drank the whole glass, after which he exclaimed, "What a cow!"

When I became archbishop of Kenya, John brought me a gift of a colorful robe from Singapore. Unfortunately, it was too tight for me, so I gave it to the archbishop of Tanzania, the most Reverend Donald Mtetemela, and it fit him perfectly. He was particularly pleased that it originated from the great John Stott.

GOD'S BRIGHT-TIED
ANGEL OF PROTECTION

MICHAEL NAZIR-ALI

Michael Nazir-Ali, from Pakistan, served in the Church of Paki-
stan and was the first bishop of Raiwind. From 1989 to 1994 he
was general secretary of the Church Mission Society, and then
bishop of Rochester until 2009, when he retired as a diocesan
bishop and took up his present position as director of the Oxford
Center for Training, Research, Advocacy and Dialogue, working
with persecuted Christians.

I have always been struck by the brightness of John's ties. However dull the day or somber the occasion, they always have a distinctly lightening effect on me (and, I am sure, on others). John
was wearing such a tie when he bounded into my room (and life)
at Ridley Hall, Cambridge, in 1970. I was then an ordinand of the
diocese of Karachi in Pakistan. My fees were paid through a bur-
sary from Ridley and the bishop of Karachi gave me a so-called
living allowance. Like so many students, making ends meet was
an interesting and precarious business! However, I was supported
by the Langham Trust (founded by John Stott in 1969 and precur-

sor of the Langham Partnership International), the Oxford Society and the Burney Fund (plus some teaching and my wife Valerie's job!) during my years of postgraduate study at Oxford and Cambridge. I was thus among the very first of that goodly fellowship of Langham Scholars that now numbers more than three hundred all over the world.

When we went to work in Pakistan, John was always ready to help with books and valuable mentoring. During our years in Karachi, Lahore and Raiwind, we seldom saw John, but it was good to know that he was there in the background. When I was appointed bishop of Raiwind in 1984, he wrote me a long letter pointing out all the pitfalls and dangers. How right he was!

John has always been passionately committed to facilitating locally rooted ministry by those he supports, but when we experienced serious and life-threatening difficulties in Pakistan, he was there to help in the transition back to England. He was delighted that an international ministry was opening up for us, first through my work for Archbishop Robert Runcie, then at the Oxford Center for Mission Studies and then for the Church Mission Society.

Throughout my years as bishop of Rochester from 1994 to 2009, John was regularly in touch with us. Always he would encourage us to keep the world, and particularly the Muslim world, in our minds, hearts and prayers. During the "severe trial" of an organized campaign against me at the time of the vacancy for the post of archbishop of Canterbury, John was a tower of strength. He was even more hurt by what was thrown at us than we were, it seemed. His prayer and practical support were unstinting, and we shall never forget it. For us, at the time, he was God's angel of protection when protection was pretty scarce.

As a personal friend, John has been most generous to us, but, of course, he has also been an authority figure to us as a mentor, teacher and scholar. Like so many others I just love the clarity of John's Bible teachings. Again and again, I turn to his commentaries for fresh, sometimes surprising insight. For example, I have been struck by the way John sees the mind of Christ mediated to the apostle Paul by the church. According to him, in the teaching about the resurrection and the Lord's Supper, for instance, Paul not only relies on his personal experience in this regard but on the testimony of the church. On questions of social and personal ethics, again and again, I turn to wisdom in collections like *Issues Facing Christians Today* as a point of departure for my own thinking.

Valerie has enjoyed and shared her discovery of John's writing on birds and people. We have, together, benefited from his teaching on Christian service, and he has again and again reminded us of God's saving purposes for the world he has created. It is amazing that someone who lived almost his entire life within a short distance of Harley Street, London (where his father was a medical practitioner), should have such a uniquely global perspective.

John always encouraged those of us who were working with the poor to be committed to bringing the whole gospel to the whole world. He knew that words should be accompanied by deeds, preaching combined with service, the pastoral sharpened by the prophetic. I believe that through the Lausanne Movement, people like John Stott, Ron Sider and Vinay Samuel were able to influence a whole generation of pastors, teachers and others to have a truly holistic view of Christian mission. For this, we are very grateful.

We praise God for the gracious work he has accomplished among us through his servant John. As John would wish, all might, majesty, dominion and praise be to the Father, the Son and the Holy Spirit, now and forever.

22

A Modern-Day Church Father

PETER KUZMIČ

Peter Kuzmič is a native of Slovenia and a citizen of Croatia, in former Yugoslavia. He cofounded and directs the Evangelical Theological Seminary in Osijek, Croatia, and is involved in many European evangelical organizations and ministries, particularly in the Balkans. Since the first Congress in 1974, he has been one of the leaders of the Lausanne Movement. He divides his time between Croatia and his teaching post at Gordon Conwell Theological Seminary, Boston.

John Stott is the most wholesome, Christlike and globally influential Christian servant-leader I have ever known. Our first substantial encounter took place at the 1974 Lausanne Congress. It was Lausanne which, more than any other event, broadened my horizons, provided me with a clear and comprehensive theological agenda, balanced my vision and energized me for holistic ministry. I was the twenty-eight-year-old principal of a two-year-old theological college in communist-dominated Yugoslavia. At that time I could not dream of platforms that would later open up to me when I would serve on the Lausanne Committee and chair its Theological Working Group after John Stott and Bishop Jack Reed.

The Lausanne Covenant became the "statement of faith" for several ministries that I was privileged to pioneer. More than once I have gratefully and proudly publicly proclaimed: *"Ich bin ein Lausanner!"*

It was at Lausanne that the world recognized John Stott as the apostle or, to put it in more secular terms, the chief engineer of evangelical unity in theological essentials and holistic mission. In his plenary presentation John laid foundations for the theme of the strategic gathering and provided definitional clarity, while resisting all temptations to evangelical triumphalism. John worked tirelessly and used his immense diplomatic skills to rescue the Congress and the global movement it launched from reductionist Western agendas, and to overcome tendencies to division and one-sided solutions proposed by other powerful voices. John was compassionate, patient and prophetic as he disarmed the critics and convinced the skeptics that God's mission was much more than just verbal proclamation. This is why many of us protest against the occasional accusation that at Lausanne John Stott "dethroned evangelism." On the contrary, many of my generation and virtually everyone in the Majority World are convinced that his role at the Congress and in writing the Lausanne Covenant actually saved the integrity of evangelical faith and witness in our cynically critical age.

Two years later (at John's initiative) we met for several days with other European evangelical theological leaders in the Belgian town of Heverlee, just outside Leuven, for a consultation on the kingdom of God and the founding of the Fellowship of European Evangelical Theologians (FEET). As we searched for a name for this new society, John in his creative, charming way convinced the rest of us, including the somewhat resistant Germans and Scandinavians, that "theology should have feet." Theologians, he argued with passion, should not be passive observers of what is going on in the world, nor should they retreat from social and political realities and hide in their secure orthodox ecclesiastical ghettos. They should dynamically and transformationally engage the kingdoms of this world on behalf of the kingdom of God.

During one of the busy breaks in that consultation, John asked me to help him compose a letter to Romanian dictator Nicolae Ceauşescu, pleading for the return of Josef Tson's recently confiscated personal library. Josef, who had gained his M.A. in Oxford, was the best-trained Baptist theologian in Romania and probably in all of Eastern Europe. He was bold and fruitful in evangelism and apologetics, and was watched closely by the communist Securitate. John could not remain indifferent when he received news of the confiscation of the valuable library of our colleague. Our letter, in which we argued that theological books were necessary tools for the trade of a pastor and appealed to the pride of a ruthless leader, resulted in a speedy return of Tson's whole library. The mix of boldness, balance and wisdom of John Stott in that process was another turning point in my own public engagement. It made me an activist for human rights, religious liberty and democracy, which in turn led to the invitation to become a founding member of the Helsinki Committee of Human Rights in my own country.

In April 1980 John came for extensive ministry in a communist-ruled country. Tito's Yugoslavia was not a member of the Soviet bloc and was relatively open to foreigners. John Stott's reputation was already well known, and I knew he would attract Christian leaders across all denominational lines. One of my students had previously translated *Basic Christianity*, and with the help of the Evangelical Literature Trust we were able to publish five thousand copies of what became the most influential primer of Christian faith in several socialist nations. In preparation for Stott's coming, evangelicals also published his booklet *Your Mind Matters*.

The central event was a well-attended "Yugoslav Lausanne," an interdenominational conference for (sadly divided) Protestant ministers, held in Novi Sad. Through the years I have interpreted for literally hundreds of speakers, among whom the most demanding were Carl Henry and Jürgen Moltmann. But translating John's lectures and sermons was a pure delight because of his organized thought and ability to express himself in clear sentences, flowing and attractive prose, and as simply as the subject matter permitted. In Novi Sad I also took the brunt of criticism from the more fundamentalist (ana)baptist brethren who had prejudices against a paedobaptist Anglican speaker and came with suspicion regarding the stated goal of searching for evangelical unity. John's clear biblical expositions, however, were accepted even by skeptical older pastors as both nourishing and enlightening. His humility, wisdom and compassion in dealing with the critical and hostile questioners disarmed most of those who were opposed to any talk of unity (except along their own reactionary and anti-ecumenical lines).

The tone set by John's talks, and the nonsectarian climate thus created, encouraged us with the founding of the first national alliance in that part of the world, the Protestant Evangelical Council. John is deservedly regarded as the godfather of this pioneering effort, which he inspired and coengineered. He served as the most authoritative adviser on procedures and policies, but above all in writing up the statement of faith. The chief drafter of that document was my former student and brother-in-law, a younger scholarly colleague and lecturer in systematic theology in Osijek, Miroslav Volf (today professor at Yale Divinity School). Miroslav still claims that John Stott's writings and personal example significantly shaped his spirituality, theology and ecumenical engagement. Subsequently most of Stott's books were translated and published in other Eastern European languages. We were proud to have his immense knowledge and skills help us pioneer in areas of theological education, Christian publishing and our search for evangelical unity.

However, it was not all work for Uncle John. He had made one condition for coming for a whole week of ministry to Yugoslavia. It was to search for rare bird species which, according to his expert knowledge, nested only in a place in southern Hungary and not far from our conference site in the wetlands of the river Danube. Miroslav and I accompanied him, equipped with binoculars, borrowed oversized rain boots and notebooks in which we recorded the names, both Latin and English, of the birds we saw. This was a doxological experience, though more for John than for Miroslav and myself. We discovered that, for John, ornithology was a subdivision, if not an actual partner, of theology. Absorbed in our explorations, however, at one point we wandered off into a forbidden area where military exercises were held. These were highly sensitive and secretive places in communist societies, and catching a foreigner there would certainly lead to lengthy investigations and possible accusations of spying, especially since we were equipped with binoculars and were making notes in a foreign language. I had started mentally to compose the text of a telegram to Frances Whitehead about why John had been arrested and how the British government should appeal for his release. Our prayers were answered, however, as we managed to slip out unobserved.

Earlier discussions of the failing Marxist vision of a new society, the abuses of totalitarian regimes, the challenges of ministry in closed societies and the need for theological training were now history due to radical political changes. John rejoiced with us when the Berlin Wall came down and Soviet Bloc countries gained freedom without any major bloodshed. He remembered the tragedies of the Budapest 1956 and Prague 1968 Soviet interventions and thanked God for Gorbachev's perestroika and glasnost policies, as well as for the Polish pope. The Lord of history used both these men to create a climate for a peaceful transition. John's lectures to our interdenominational and international student body are still talked about, literally around the world. Several of his listeners subsequently became Langham Scholars and leaders in theological education, well-known churchmen and public leaders. There is no doubt that John Stott helped us to pioneer evangelical theological enterprises and Christian public engagement in several (post)communist East European nations and beyond. His powerful expositions and his plea for unity and cooperation at the conference of evangelical theological leaders in Oradea, Romania, in 1993, led to the establishment of the Council for Theological Education in Eastern Europe, a pioneering effort that bore other fruit in the postcommunist world.

But he also made a more personal impact. My first sabbatical was made possible by John, who arranged a semester in Cambridge for me and my family, residing at Tyndale House. I remember how surprised my family was by the small car in which John picked us up at the airport and drove us to Cambridge. We had flown into Heathrow from Los Angeles after a semester of teaching in California, where my children got the wrong idea that all Christian leaders drive big cars. It was a wonderful opportunity to teach them about the importance of a simple lifestyle and to introduce them to Ron Sider's *Rich Christians in an Age of Hunger.* Their conviction that John was a genuine follower of Jesus was further confirmed when we once visited him in his small London flat. Uncle John became a favorite among my kids because of his obvious love for children and his charming sense of humor. Once when I expressed my envy of his literary output, he graciously pointed to my daughters—small girls at that time—for whom, he said, he envied me.

I have watched closely John's concern about growing militarism and the arms race, about death and destruction, about injustices and exploitation in the economic order of the world, about the violation of human rights and discrimination, but above all his pain about the plight of the poor and the weak. His concern for the well-being of every human being (insisting that all are made in the image of God) was obvious even in the way he treated people we met on the street or waitresses in various restaurants. John encouraged many of us to evangelize, because people everywhere were lost apart from Christ's saving work. He himself was a passionate evangelist, fully aware of the deep consequences of human falseness both for individuals and human communities. He strongly believed in the liberating power of the gospel and responsible freedom under the lordship of Christ. At the same time, he constantly encouraged us not to give up dreaming of a world in which hatred would be replaced by love, revenge by forgiveness, war by peace, slavery by freedom, and enmity by reconciliation. John's ability to articulate this vision in the light of the gospel rather than any human ideology, and to see the church as "God's new society," was an inspiration to many of us. He modeled biblical Christianity: what it means to think critically, live credibly and proclaim joyfully the transformative message of the Lord Jesus Christ.

These are some of the reasons why we evangelicals in Eastern Europe consider John Stott not only our friend and facilitator of ministries, but also view him as a veritable modern-day church father.

23

The Founding of John Stott Ministries in the United States

DEE DEE MacLEAN

*Dee Dee MacLean was instrumental in the founding of the Lang-
ham Foundation, which later became John Stott Ministries in
the United States, and was a member of the board until 2001.
Now retired, she lives in Illinois.*

God often snatches extremely unlikely people to share in his
service. No record of John Stott's ministry in the United States is
adequate without portraits of two couples: Bouton and Winnie
McDougal, and Wells and Florence Farnham. They were instrumental in the formation of the Langham Foundation in the United
States, which later changed its name (rather against John's own
wishes) to John Stott Ministries—the American member of the
Langham Partnership International.

Bouton McDougal had been a napalm-tongued attorney with a
large, prestigious law firm (Sidley and Austin), whom God allured
by the Christian testimony and transformed lives of two of his
teenage children. Sweet, bright Winnie joined him in the faith.
Fruit followed prolifically. Having retired, Bouton accepted the

leadership of the Chicago Sunday Evening Club, a weekly television hour. He transformed it from a liberal, largely Unitarian program into a splendid proclamation, with Scripture, music, testimonies and leading evangelical speakers, including John Stott.

Florence Farnham was married to Wells, the cofounder of a large investment firm (Stein, Roe and Farnham). Wells was a man of quiet, wry humor (he once observed that "a Christian is someone who thinks nobody else is"). Florence was an ebullient, gregarious lady who burst forth with evangelistic zeal in very creative ways. She hosted elegant soirées at which John Stott spoke. John always stayed with the Farnhams when in the Chicago area, ensconced in what Florence dubbed her "Prophet's Chamber."

When I was teaching in upstate New York, early one Sunday morning in the 1960s I sleepily happened onto a radio program, part of a four-week series sponsored by a mainline denomination. To my astonishment (because of its usual liberal bent), the speaker that day was electrifying—sound in doctrine and powerful. It was John Stott. It was about ten years later that I discovered it had been Florence Farnham who was behind the choice of John Stott for that series.

My own exposure to John Stott's teaching slowly continued. Some of my students attended an Urbana Student Missions Convention and proclaimed the best part to be the Bible studies by John Stott, and they brought tapes to prove it. I had read most of John's books by the time I visited All Souls in 1964. Later, in 1971 when Trinity Evangelical Divinity School (TEDS) awarded him an honorary doctorate, John preached on Psalm 32. As always, he was clear and memorable.

So it was that in the fall of 1972, the McDougals and the Farnhams were among the four hundred or so who more than filled the missions room at TEDS each week for an exposition of the Sermon on the Mount by John Stott, and that was how I met them. Florence Farnham was almost sitting in my lap when chairs were squeezed in to accommodate an overflow, and her expansive personality enveloped me. The next year she invited me to a dinner at which John was present, and in January 1974 she dragooned me into driving him to Wheaton College to speak, and then on to downtown Chicago to the offices of Sidley and Austin for the legal conception of the Langham Foundation.

Bouton McDougal insisted that the new organization should be legally incorporated, so that people could support John Stott's worldwide ministry tax deductibly. He challenged Wells Farnham to donate a certain amount—an amount which, amusingly, was double what he himself planned to give (because, as he commented, though Wells was older, Bouton was already retired). Wells was delighted to comply with this request, and so with this generous financial midwifery, the Langham Foundation was birthed in December 1974.

These four dear friends are all now with the Lord, but what they planted has burgeoned wonderfully. The Langham Foundation, later called John Stott Ministries, has grown to be a major contributing member of the Langham Partnership International, whose programs support and strengthen churches, pastors and seminaries all around the world. They themselves were glorious symbols of what John's ministry conveys: the One who makes all things new is an earnest seeker of the flamboyant, the wary, the incendiary—whatever—and transforms them into people who resemble himself. Such were the progenitors of the Langham Foundation!

THE BOY WITH
THE DISAPPEARING EYES

DAVID JONES

David Jones first met John Stott while serving as president of Scripture Union, USA. He later served for ten years as the first president of John Stott Ministries, the U.S. wing of the Langham Partnership International. He and John Stott traveled together throughout the United States from approximately 1993 until 2005. David is now president of Strive, a ministry advisory firm, which has headquarters in Colorado, where he also lives.

For many years I had the joy and privilege of traveling with John Stott on his frequent trips to the United States, and also on a number of his visits to the Global South. These outings started when I was president of Scripture Union and then continued during my ten years as president of John Stott Ministries. During these trips, I had a wonderful opportunity to get to know Uncle John in a variety of unique settings and circumstances.

Perhaps one of the less well-known characteristics of John Stott was his wonderful sense of humor. This was a trait frequently on display during his travels. All who have met him in person will remember his pleasant smile, rosy cheeks and sparkling eyes, whenever something amusing is said. John himself recalls that his school friends referred to him as the "boy with the disappearing eyes," as his eyes would narrow to a squint whenever he smiled or laughed. Friends and close colleagues have heard him say many funny things over the years, but I have only a couple of times seen him really "crack up."

John Stott was a great "kidder" and would test the boldness of new acquaintances (and his study assistants!) by doing some surprising things, such as

- jumping over railings at the entrance of restaurants
- ordering the strangest things at meals ("I think the 'Rooty Tooty Fresh and Fruity' sounds just marvelous")
- splashing new friends while washing dishes with them

This last prank on the list was a rite of passage for new friends helping Uncle John in the kitchen. He would spring up from the table and offer to wash the dishes if his new friend would agree to dry them. Then, he would figure out how to drop the dish into the rinsing water at just the right angle to ensure that his kitchen partner would get soaked! It was amazing how long some folks would endure this before saying something about it. Then Uncle John would look rather innocent and say, "I am so sorry. Was I getting you wet?" And then his eyes would disappear in laughter.

Uncle John loved Americans, but he also really enjoyed teasing them. Only he could get away with a joke like this one: "What's the difference between a cow chewing its cud and an American chewing gum? The intelligent look on the cow." However, I had the chance to return the favor a few times. One such opportunity was when I greeted him in Philadelphia after a flight from London. He was often pleased, surprised and even baffled by the ways that Americans would work a gospel message into normal, everyday events. So, this time, I greeted him with a new product I had picked up at a Christian bookstore, called "Test-a-Mints": it was a roll of mints with a Bible verse printed on the side of each one (Testamints, get it?). I offered him a mint and soberly explained the remarkable gospel outreach opportunity that this product presented. I waited for his response. After a few moments of wondering what to say, he smiled and said, "Most remarkable!" I then told him *his* verse was "the wages of sin is death." Realizing now that I was kidding him, he quipped, "The wages of a *kidder's* sin is to carry my luggage to the car!"

During his trips to the United States, he was often introduced by American pastors before he spoke. Sometimes they would embarrass him with the length and detail and flattery of their introduction. Here is one story he liked to tell:

> I was introduced by a rather large pastor from Florida some years ago. He was indeed a big man and it had likely been some years since he saw his feet! After a very long introduction, he ended with the flourish: "I would crawl on my knees, 500 miles, just to hear John Stott speak." [And hearing Uncle John say this with a southern accent was as funny as the rest of the story.]
>
> The pastor finally relinquished his pulpit, exited the platform, sat down in the front row, and after a minute or two, fell soundly asleep! Not only did he fall asleep, he began to snore—loudly! [Then, after a superbly timed pause for comic effect . . .] I can only assume that the poor man was utterly exhausted from his 500-mile crawl!

Now, on to the times when he really "cracked up"! Uncle John did not enjoy televised interviews or times when he was asked to do a video clip in support of a project or ministry. He much preferred interacting directly with people—and the cameras made the whole process "a bit artificial," as he would say. After some prodding, he was persuaded to do a quick video to promote an effort to support scholarships for top church leaders in the Global South. Unfortunately, the video camera was not working as it should, and the "brief" video project had lengthened to twenty minutes, then thirty minutes. He was willing to continue, but by now the spontaneity of the moment was gone and he was getting weary.

I was coaching him to smile during the piece, which ended with the phrase "Won't you please join us?" Well, at last the video camera cooperated, and Uncle John soldiered on through the piece, but I noticed that his face was gloomily devoid of his usual pleasant smile, rosy cheeks and sparkling eyes. He came to the final line, said the closing words "Won't you please join us?"—and then broke into the most enormous smile! It was such a shock that the whole production crew immediately burst out laughing. Gasping for air in the midst of his own laughter (complete with tears running down his face), Uncle John looked at me and said, "Well, DJ, you told me to say, 'Won't you please join us' and smile—and that is exactly what I did!" I didn't think of my directions as being in chronological order—but that was how Uncle John took it. Like the trooper he is, once everyone had stopped laughing, he recorded a flawless message, but I will never forget the huge smile on his face and the laughter that followed!

Anyone who has spent time with Uncle John knows of his love of the stories of H. H. Munro, an Edwardian writer of short stories, who used the nom de plume of Saki. One of his favorite Saki stories is titled "The Storyteller."[1]

A few years ago, an anonymous benefactor enabled my wife and daughter and me to accompany John Stott and his study assistant on a voyage aboard the *Sea Cloud*, an amazing wooden sailing yacht, often used by Christian groups for memorable voyages. Uncle John was promised that he would not have to speak or lecture, and was assured that this was truly a vacation for him. But once the passengers found out that he was aboard, he was asked to "do something, anything so our folks can hear you."

After some discussion, we negotiated a formal reading of Saki. I am not sure what the passengers were expecting, but they soon found out that Saki was not a revered theologian, but a humor writer (somewhat in the style of P. G. Wodehouse)! I had watched Uncle John read this story several times—and he could never get through it without starting to laugh at one particular point. The story is about a little girl who was awarded medals for her good behavior. In the words of Saki:

> She was so good . . . that she won several medals for good-ness, which she always wore, pinned on to her dress. There was a medal for obedience, another medal for punctuality, and a third for good behavior. They were large metal medals and they clicked against one another as she walked. No other child in the town where she lived had as many as three med-als, so everybody knew that she must be an extra good child.

Have you ever noticed that things are funnier when you have a sense of what is coming next? Well, I knew that Uncle John was going to have a tough time getting through the next section of the story—as it contained the line that always made him laugh. And the response of his *Sea Cloud* audience was already boisterous—they were really enjoying the story and John's reading of it.

The moment of truth was approaching. Uncle John then read the words:

> Bertha walked up and down and enjoyed herself immensely, and thought to herself: "If I were not so extraordinarily good I should not have been allowed to come into this beautiful park and enjoy all that there is to be seen in it," and her three medals clinked against one another as she walked and helped to remind her how very good she really was.

Uncle John read this line and then tried to say the one that followed. He started giggling. The audience laughed harder. He started laughing. The audience burst into even louder laughter. He tried several more times to get back into the story, but to no avail. Finally, he took off his glasses, removed his handkerchief to clean them and, raising them to his eyes to look at the lenses, said, "I have laughed so hard, I have fogged up my spectacles." At that, the audience roared uncontrollably, and it was several more minutes before he was able to finish his story!

I can't ever remember laughing as long and as hard. Uncle John said later that his ribs still hurt from Saki!

"The boy with the disappearing eyes" grew up to be a remarkable servant of God, who continued to have that pleasant smile, rosy cheeks and sparkling eyes—and a great sense of humor.

THE LANGHAM PARTNERSHIP IS BORN

CHRIS WRIGHT

Chris Wright is from Northern Ireland; after five years teaching the Old Testament in India, he worked from 1989 until 2001 at All Nations Christian College, England, as academic dean and then principal. In 2001 he was invited by John Stott to become the first international director of the Langham Partnership International, which combined several ministries John Stott had founded thirty years earlier. He and his wife, Liz, live in London.

Chris, preserve your independence." Those were the first words of advice I ever heard from John Stott, and they have stuck with me and steadied me through my life. I was having tea with him and my wife, Liz, in his Bridford Mews flat, having climbed the winding stairs with some trepidation, like others before and after me. He had invited me after our first personal encounter during the National Evangelical Conference on Social Ethics (NECSE) at High Leigh in 1978, when I was just thirty-one and he was in the prime of his leadership at fifty-seven. I had completed my Ph.D. in Old Testament social ethics the previous year, and those were the days of exciting ferment in the wake of the Lausanne

Congress of 1974. Younger evangelicals like myself were keen to see a reengagement of our biblical faith with the surrounding culture in all its social, economic and political dimensions. John Stott was our hero in that flush of activity that saw the founding of the original *Third Way* magazine (at that time rooted in the Lausanne Covenant) and campaigning organizations like the Festival of Light, the Shaftesbury Project, TEAR Fund (now Tearfund), and then the Jubilee Center and the London Institute for Contemporary Christianity.

I had been invited to give one of the Bible expositions at NECSE, which I did on Psalm 86, with John sitting in the back row. Afterward, he was kind enough to speak to me approvingly of how I had handled the text in a balanced way, and sat down with me for lunch. As with so many others, there followed that gentle interrogation about my past, present and future, the invitation to tea, and the beginning of a lifelong friendship.

In our tea-time conversation, I expressed how frustrated I had already become with the polarization of evangelicals over their theology of social engagement: some advocated a "creation" approach and a rather conservative agenda, while others trumpeted "kingdom ethics" and a more radical "jubilee" drive to change the underlying structures of injustice in society. It seemed to me that both were in danger of shortcut biblical hermeneutics, when in fact each approach necessarily involved the other in any comprehensive biblical theology. "I find I can't agree fully with either side or simply toe a party line," I said. That was when I received his advice, "Preserve your independence," by which I think he meant that I should continue to think for myself, come to my own convictions from the Bible and not just take sides in the typical tribal allegiances of evangelicalism. Since then, while I continue to rejoice in the term *evangelical*—in its rich content and history—I would always put "being biblical" above "being evangelical," a hierarchy that I think John himself would endorse. For if some would lament that the church is not evangelical enough, my complaint would be that evangelicals are often not biblical enough.

Shortly afterward, he invited me to consider going to teach the Old Testament in Trinity Theological College, Singapore. I went to tea again. I found the courage to "preserve my independence" and say no, because I wanted to complete a good period of years in pastoral ministry as a curate in Tonbridge Parish Church, Kent, before going into theological education, possibly overseas. I believe it was the one and only time I ever declined an invitation from John Stott! But it did nothing to damage our friendship or his interest in my ministry and our growing young family. For when I did later end up teaching for five years at the Union Biblical Seminary in India, from 1983-1988, he corresponded regularly with us—always remembering our children.

While we were there, he stayed briefly at the seminary during one of his long international trips, along with his then study assistant, Toby Howarth. One afternoon he came for a meal to our home on the campus. The outstanding memory of those hours was how, as soon as our children came into the room, he greeted each of them by name, and then spent time ignoring Liz and me, and giving full attention to chatting with them at their own level about their interests. The next morning he was to go birdwatching on the banks of the Mula-Mutha River, which flows through Pune, and since our younger son Jonathan at twelve years old was (I confess with shame) the only member of the family interested in birds at that time, he got hold of an old fogged-up pair of binoculars and went with John's party at first light. He tells us he spotted some birds that even John didn't see, and still counts it as some claim to fame that "I went birding with John Stott before my dad." The same Jonathan now works for the Royal Society for the Protection of Birds, to John Stott's delight.

We returned from India in 1988, and I began a thirteen-year stretch on the staff of All Nations Christian College, first as academic dean, and then as principal. Even before we came home, however, John Stott's legendary watchfulness over those he was mentoring swung into play, and he had written to me with two invitations. One was to take over from Vinay Samuel the leadership of the Theological Resource Team of EFAC—the Evangelical Fellowship in the Anglican Communion (another international network founded by John himself). That led to fourteen years of convening small international consultations in different parts of the world, out of which arose many friendships in the Majority World that have been a great blessing to me and a rich reservoir of friendships when I later moved into my current roles in Langham and Lausanne. The mere fact of representing an organization that was founded and endorsed by John Stott guaranteed a kind of reflected glow of warmth, friendship and cooperation. I think that must be one of his greatest contributions to the world church—intangible though it is—that his own unbounded capacity for genuine friendships all around the world multiplied and enriched whole new generations of consequential friendships among hundreds of others, some of them very dear and deep. It is a beautiful human legacy with God's fingerprints all over it.

The other invitation was to join the board of trustees of the Evangelical Literature Trust (ELT), the charity founded by John as a means of channeling all his own royalties and other donated funds into providing books for pastors and seminaries in the Majority World. It was a joy to work with people like John Hayden, Nigel Sylvester, David Spence, David Cansdale and others in this literature project that few people knew about but was having an immensely beneficial effect all around the world. Later I became the chair of the literature committee of ELT, and at one point I invited Pieter Kwant to join us and give us the benefit of his professional expertise, range of contacts in the publishing world and knowledge of many parts of the Majority World, especially Africa. Out of those friendships and relationships eventually emerged

what is now Langham Literature, one of the three constituent programs of the Langham Partnership International—a development
that John Stott observed, approved and greeted with evident delight and encouragement. For me, however, during those thirteen
years when we lived in rural Hertfordshire, it gave me regular ex-
cuses to make the journey to Warren Street tube station (little
dreaming that one day I would live round the corner), walk to the
basement at 12 Weymouth Street and be greeted with John's hearty
handshake and customary hug, and get down to business with the
committee, under the watchful eye (as I now know) of Frances
Whitehead. Those sessions were supplemented by John's further
invitation to join Christian Debate, read all kinds of books and
enjoy stimulating discussion with other friends of John, fortified
by the legendary quiche, coleslaw, cherry tomatoes, orange squash
and ice cream.

Getting to know John more and more, enjoying his friendship
and admiring his leadership—that was one thing. Being asked to
take over from him—that was something else altogether. In late
1999 I was beginning to wonder if I should remain at All Nations
(I was very happy and fulfilled in leadership there) or seek some
new context for ministry. Trusting in John's wisdom and confi-
dentiality, I wrote a long letter to him, sharing my concerns, interests and hopes, and seeking his counsel. Yet another invitation to
tea ensued for Liz and myself.

It turned out that John and some of his friends were wondering
what future lay ahead for his ministries as he himself, approaching
his eighties, was needing to withdraw from active leadership of
them. Could it be that I should take over some of that leadership
role? A consultation was called together to consider the future of
the Langham Trust, and the Evangelical Literature Trust particularly, both of which now had international connections, supporters
and agents. Two things were agreed: that there needed to be greater
structural coordination of all these ministries, even while there

should be some degree of decentralizing from the control hitherto exercised from Weymouth Street, and that somebody should be appointed to oversee that transition and pull it all together, exercising at least some of the role that John had played (without in any sense being considered as replacing the irreplaceable).

The time came when John explicitly asked me to be that person. He took me for a meal in DeMartino's Italian restaurant on Great Portland Street (one of his favorites). I remember asking him two questions: "What will it involve?" and "Why me?" Actually, I don't remember getting a clear answer to either question, perhaps because none of us could predict any answer to the first, and perhaps because the second had no answer beyond John's lifelong ability just to "know" who he wanted in particular roles, and to trust his own judgment and the Lord's guidance. However, I went home that night reassured in my heart that it was a right move for me, even if my questions remained real ones for some time. More painful was the fact that John resolutely declined my offer to walk home with him (already his eyesight was treacherous and he was tending to bump into things), and I could do no other than bid him goodnight on the street. The next time I saw him he had an enormous black eye, and it turned out he had tripped over a bollard (or post) on his way home that evening, and narrowly missed being run over on Great Portland Street. I wince still as I think of it.

Langham Partnership International was formed in the spring of 2001, and Liz and I moved to London in August of that year, on our wedding anniversary, for me to take up the post of international director. We moved to a house just five minutes' walk from John's flat, ten minutes from All Souls Church—a deliberate move into the orbit of both. On the evening of the day we moved, John insisted on treating our whole family, along with his study assistant Corey Widmer and his wife, Sarah (who had gallantly helped us in the move), to a meal in another Italian restaurant. We didn't dare look at the bill as he picked it up, but just marveled, with so many others, at his amazing thoughtfulness and generosity. He was genuinely delighted to have us, as he put it, as his near neighbors.

In the autumn of 2001 John had already arranged a tour of Peru and Argentina for some preaching seminars, arranged by Samuel Escobar and René Padilla. He wanted me to accompany him, believing that this should be the beginning of another Langham ministry, alongside Literature and Scholars (it was eventually consolidated as Langham Preaching, under the leadership of Jonathan Lamb). So we traveled together, encountering all the awful hassles of air travel in the immediate post-9/11 world. How I came to admire the sheer grit of this wiry old gentleman sitting beside me, struggling through endless queues and the indignities of security searches, cramped in economy seating, coping with lack of sleep and jet lag, refusing to use a stick, even though his feet no longer obeyed him as they should. John was utterly determined to keep going in his preaching and teaching and encouraging ministries, no matter what physical demands it made on his rugged but battered constitution. He had already celebrated his eightieth birthday, as he reminded a young lady at the reception desk of an airport lounge in Miami. "I'm an octogenarian, you know," he said. "You're a *what?*" she replied with utter lack of interest.

In Argentina we shared a room for the week, and he continued his daily habit of early rising for Bible study and prayer, in which I joined him, eased just a little by the ruse of allowing him to use the bathroom first, after the alarm went off. One night, however, I wanted to get to preparation for my teaching as early as possible, so I asked if I might use the bathroom first the next morning. That would be fine, he said, as he adjusted and set his little travel alarm clock. The alarm went off and I shuffled over to the bathroom, and found myself rubbing my eyes in the shower, wondering why I felt still half asleep and thick-headed. I emerged to find my saintly roommate sitting forlorn and shrunken in his pajamas on the edge of his bed. "Chris," he murmured apologetically, "I'm afraid we have made a mistake. It's 4:20 a.m." He had set his alarm for 4:00 a.m. instead of his then customary 6:00 a.m. I felt more sorry for him than for myself, though I resisted the temptation to climb straight back into bed. I think he did, though.

Our travels together continued, with two grueling coast-to-coast tours of Australia in 2002 (brilliantly organized by Wendy Toulmin) and Canada in 2003 (equally well arranged by Elizabeth Denbeigh) to promote the work of the Langham Partnership in those countries. Our last international trip, with quite a posse of others, was to China and Hong Kong in early 2006. Wherever we went on these tours, or for events in the United Kingdom, John would introduce me as his successor, with lavish and embarrassing flattery—but so sincerely articulated that I could never get him to change it. In any case, he would say, flattery is like cigarette smoke; it does you no harm so long as you don't inhale. I could only respond, when people talked about what an awesome task I had taken on, that there was no way that I felt myself to be a successor to John Stott *himself*—the man was utterly unique and irreplaceable. Rather I was being tasked and entrusted with the *vision* God had given to John Stott and the ministries he had founded. And that was something I could wholeheartedly throw myself into for love of him and the Lord we both serve.

The steady consolidation and growth of Langham Partnership International gave John constantly articulated pleasure and whatever kind of rightful pride we are allowed in the Christian life. As long as he could, he continued to attend board meetings, but from the moment of my appointment he insisted that I was the leader and he would not seek to dictate what I should do or how things should be run. He was as good as his word. We met regularly in his flat for breakfast (until he moved to the College of St. Barnabas in 2007, where I continued to visit him), and I felt rather like I imagine Timothy felt when he had to report to the apostle Paul. After our muesli and toast, we cleared the table and got out our notebooks and diaries. He would have a list of issues to discuss with me, and he expected me to have a matching one. He rejoiced in every good report and would have words of encouragement and advice on problems and concerns. But never, ever was there any pulling of rank, demands or criticism. Then we would pray together and get on with the day ahead. It was a most beautiful, liberating and affirming relationship, and a delightful privilege for which I am immensely grateful to God.

After several years in leadership of Langham Partnership International, I think I could give a fuller answer to my first question, "What will it involve?" But the second still causes me to wonder with humble amazement, "Why me?"

WIDER INTERESTS

BIRDING BEFORE DAWN
AROUND THE WORLD

PETER HARRIS

Peter and Miranda Harris founded the Christian conservation organization A Rocha, in Portugal in 1983. John Stott was on its first Council of Reference and went birding often with the Harrises. Since then, A Rocha International has grown to include work in twenty countries, and Peter is its president. Peter and Miranda, after years of living in Portugal and France, now live in the United Kingdom.

It had all come as something of a surprise. Despite the fact that rather few British Christians seemed to be taking the known crisis in the world's ecosystems to heart, the Universities and Colleges Christian Fellowship (UCCF) had decided to sponsor our ornithological trip to southern Sweden, their first environmental initiative. It was 1982, and in the face of a certain amount of evangelical muttering, we thought it was prudent to recruit some irreproachable theological support. I had only met John Stott once before, two years earlier, when he had come to bless the graduating class of ordinands and other students from Trinity College,

Bristol, but his passion for birding was well known. Given his increasingly direct appeals for contemporary application of biblical Christian thinking, we had some hope that he would give us a sympathetic hearing for our ideas. I was, however, completely unprepared for the fact that he was so immediately interested. John's letters are the kind you keep, and so I still have this letter with the others: "I am so glad the Falsterbo expedition to watch the raptor migration was such a success—I wish I could have joined you!"

So he never made it on that trip, but he did agree immediately to join the Council of Reference of the A Rocha Trust to which it gave birth. Once again, it was on conditions we had not expected, but which we came to know as characteristic. He wrote:

> I made a decision some years ago that, as a matter of integrity, I would not be on any council of reference unless I was personally involved in the work concerned, and thus able to speak from personal knowledge about it. Indeed, only these last two or three weeks I have declined a couple of invitations on this ground. . . . Perhaps I should insist on your inviting me to visit the field study center and bird observatory in Portugal [A Rocha] at the earliest possible moment!! Will you be coming to London during the early months of the New Year? Then perhaps we could meet and talk and my conscience would permit me to accept your invitation.

We did meet. He did come to Portugal. And it proved to be the start of a friendship and a collaboration that lasted over a quarter of a century, even though it came at a time of his life when he was already deeply committed to many other organizations around the world.

At first we saw our role as perhaps providing the way for John to lay down some of the more major demands of his life. In doing birding in the spare moments of his travels, he was able to keep his legendary mental powers in gear, but he was then applying it to problems such as how to determine the length of the Bee-eaters' nest hole, rather than the more intractable challenges of whether the Anglican Church was thinking straight about ordaining women bishops, or how evangelical Christian leaders around the world could reconcile their newly recovered social conscience with their convictions about the vital work of preaching and evangelism.

Even our own somewhat spontaneous family life seemed to be a welcome distraction on his first stay with us in our rented accommodation in Portugal. He arrived late one evening when our youngest daughter, Bethan, was just three weeks old, and Miranda's *feijoada*[1] was about to burn on the stove as John came over the doorstep. Miranda's request, "Could you hold her a moment?" didn't prove a challenge to this particular bachelor. He simply called on years of baptismal experience and took Bethan in his arms. He showed equal abilities with small children and struck up rapid friendships with all of ours. He developed a series of competitions with our son Jeremy, who at the ripe age of four had just broken his arm by tripping over on the rough track by our house. They culminated in John secretly signing Jem's plaster cast while he slept on the morning John left at his accustomed early hour. I would have come close to burnout if I had ever attempted to keep up with the rhythms of life that were a simple routine for John.

However, John's ease with predawn hours equipped him to be the perfect companion on a series of birding trips over successive years. The trick was to find a place at the end of one of his speaking tours and convene there for a week or so, usually with a couple of other friends, but with only one guiding principle—the birding came first in all the decisions. So the accommodation was frequently lamentable, the food infrequent and occasionally high risk, but John's delight in what he saw and his stamina in getting to the places where some of the more remote species were to be found made everything worthwhile. We were fortunate that experts such as Rick and Barbara Mearns could come with us to Turkey and Spain, and in the United States Rob and Helen Kelsh were able to join us. Colin Jackson of A Rocha Kenya also had a spectacular week in Ethiopia with John, continuing the tradition, and Ginny Vroblesky of A Rocha USA went down to Belize for another trip. But mostly it was Miranda and I who had the joy of planning an itinerary that would take John out of the stress of his normal travels and into the close study of what he taught us to understand as "God's book of works"—the companion volume to God's book of words, the Bible, in God's revelation.

There are stories of course.

There was the time when Sunday worship conflicted gravely with raptor migration across the Straits of Gibraltar, the wind having swung to the west shortly after dawn, bringing low-flying black kites distractingly close as we went into the church. "Don't I recognize you?" said the minister musingly and hospitably, as we tried to do a rapid exit after the early service. "Just visiting bird-watchers, . . ." muttered John Stott evasively, pulling down his cap and looking shifty as he tried to avoid recognition and the inevitable delaying conversation that would ensue.

Then, on the northern edges of the Sahara in Morocco (blue-cheeked bee-eater, hoopoe lark, houbara bustard, but we never did find Dupont's lark) it was still oppressively hot one evening, and John was in determined mood as we searched for a cool place to eat. Others of his traveling companions must know what that steely will could mean, even if its intentions were invariably expressed in the most courteous of terms. So the owner of the only place worth patronizing in the village, but who had set up his café in a stuffy downstairs room, found himself part of an unstoppable mission to find some ropes from a neighbor and then haul his table and chairs up onto the flat roof so we could eat under the stars and in the breeze. By the end of the meal John and his collaborator had assumed the demeanor of coconspirators against the feeble ambitions of the rest of us, and a new business idea had been launched. I wonder if people still eat up there on that roof?

The need for John to get his legendary HHH (horizontal half hour) after lunch was never too much of a problem either. He could sleep anywhere and regularly did. He seriously needed to do so since he was usually up by 4:30 a.m., and we couldn't always honor the day's planned endings around 10 p.m. if the traveling got away from us. Apparently the crucial component of success, should the appointed hour for his HHH arrive when we were out on some hillside, was that he should be able to dig a hole for his hip so that he could sleep comfortably on his side. Cold or heat weren't considerations, and neither was the hardness of the ground; nothing would prevent him either from dropping off to sleep as soon as he lay down, or from waking up exactly thirty minutes later.

Even on his holidays, his self-discipline and determination were astonishing. During a visit to northern Turkey in 1993, he was working on his commentary on the epistle to the Romans. It was causing him some genuine intellectual anguish because he had resolved to take to heart the many approaches found in other commentaries and had been assimilating the diverse views of over thirty other authors, several of whom seemed to him to be undermining the very foundations of the gospel to which he had resolutely committed his life. In order to cope with the challenge, he had given himself the challenge of working for at least an hour on his script every day of the year except Sundays. Once again we had ended up late the previous evening in a fairly basic hostel—this time on a lakeshore where we hoped the following morning to find red-breasted flycatchers and rosefinches among many other migrants (we did, together with an awesome migration of lesser-spotted eagles and great flocks of white pelicans). It was cold, and the rather public latrines gave the whole place a pervasively unhealthy smell. When Miranda and I stumbled out of bed around 6 a.m., it was to find John emerging glowing from his unheated room, wrapped head to food in a blanket, deeply satisfied by the logic of the apostle Paul and content that his morning's writing had done it justice.

John never saw any part of his life as without purpose, and on every trip we saw time and again the way that a straightforward concern for everyone was a consistent part of his thinking, feeling and decision making. On one occasion he was beginning a speaking tour round the United States as we were finishing some teaching in Vancouver, and so we agreed to meet in Oregon to take as much ornithological advantage as we could from this happy overlap. Despite his jet lag, after having just arrived from Europe and having planned the usual 6 a.m. departure for the next day's search for Lewis's woodpecker, he stayed up until well after midnight, talking over the questions about Christian belief that were bothering one of our hosts. On a later trip to Romania, another arduous proposition for one who by then was in his mid-seventies, in the biting cold of December (his speaking itinerary didn't always give us the most congenial of venues for birding—but yes, we did find the red-breasted geese which were the whole point as far as John was concerned), he gave a lot of time to preparing some teaching for the pastor and his wife with whom we were staying. We noticed for the first time, on that occasion, how he had the ability to "go turbo" mentally when he needed to, and yet with his advancing years, to husband his energy when required. It was on that trip too that we witnessed his extraordinarily moving meeting with a church leader, who was by then president of his denomination, and had risked imprisonment during the communist years in order to smuggle John's books around the country.

Over the years his involvement with A Rocha became steadily greater. He helped us formulate a solid theological basis for the work we were doing and joined us in several countries to plead with Christian leaders the cause of caring for creation. He wrote articles and forewords for our publications and advised us on the wisdom of different alliances and against potential distractions. I believe his own thinking was able to take shape through the challenge of seeing several of the practical conservation projects that A Rocha people were undertaking in places as diverse as Lebanon, Kenya and Southall in the United Kingdom. He helped us identify some wonderful leaders from the non-Western nonwhite world, and he made it his business to turn them into what he called "ornitheologians."

We will miss him greatly—his gift for close friendship with Miranda and myself, his genuine interest in our family, the welcomes to his tiny London flat to plan the next trip over sandwiches provided by the equally indefatigable Frances, his knowledgeable delight in all he saw that was familiar, and his endless penetrating questions about anything that was new to him. The simplicity of his lifestyle was a constant reminder of his many friends around the world who lived in tough and needy circumstances, and whom he always kept in his mind and in his (meticulously organized) praying. He was a great field companion and a true Christian—probably more profoundly converted than anyone else I have known.

The Call of the Loon

MARK HUNT

*Mark Hunt lives in Michigan and grew up knowing John Stott
through his parents, Keith and Gladys Hunt. In 1973 John Stott
invited him to come and work at All Souls, Langham Place, for a
year, and in 1976 John officiated at Mark and Marian's wedding.
Mark has served on several boards of ministries established by
John Stott, and after years working in the field of Christian publishing for Zondervan, he joined the staff of the Langham Partnership International as International Operations Director in
2008.*

John Stott became part of our family in 1956. Stacey Woods,
then general secretary of InterVarsity Christian Fellowship (IVCF),
had invited him to come to North America and do a series of missions at several universities. After some initial reluctance, John
agreed and came for three months, thinking at the time that perhaps he might never come back to America. This was his first international speaking tour, and my father was assigned the role of
hosting John throughout his time in America. A friendship was
struck that has continued for more than fifty years, one that soon
included our entire family. I was a young boy at this time, but

from my earliest memories I recall my parents speaking of John Stott with great admiration, and the occasional meetings with this pleasant but awe-inspiring rosy-cheeked man.

The early meetings grew into a fuller friendship and spawned opportunities to work alongside John. On reflection I feel a bit like the character Zelig in the Woody Allen film, who keeps appearing in the background of historical world events. As a student I attended the 1967 Urbana Student Missions Convention at which John gave Bible readings on 2 Timothy (I still meet people who can recall this series and its impact on their life), and then the 1970 Urbana where he spoke on the Upper Room discourse. In 1972, when John returned to the University of Michigan and the site of one of his 1956 lectures, I attended his lectures on Christ the controversialist. During that weekend John graciously invited me to go to London and spend a year working with the staff of All Souls Church; I could not have begun to imagine the impact this would have on my life. During that year, 1973, preparations for the historic Lausanne Congress were in full swing. In later years I played small roles in what became John Stott Ministries in the United States and then in the founding of Langham Partnership International.

John's impact on the global church is profound. But my immediate thoughts of John come from the times we went birding together.

In the autumn of 1973, John asked if I would care to join him for a few hours of birding at a London waterworks (many years later, I am not exactly sure where we went but I think it may have been Barn Elms). I was still building my list of U.K. birds and thought it would be good to spend some time preparing by memorizing the ducks we would be likely to see, and then for good measure I committed a few of the scientific Latin names to memory as well. The following morning, as we walked along the shores, I exclaimed, "Look, John, an *Anas stepera*!"[1] John slowly lowered his binoculars, looked at me and said, "Really?" before resuming his search for ducks of real interest. He never lacked a response for any situation.

In the early 1970s, John spent two weeks at Cedar Campus, IVCF's training center in northern Michigan, on the shore of Lake Huron. He was eager to find the nesting site of the common loon (known in the United Kingdom as the northern diver). As the loon is rather shy, this led to several expeditions into the woods in search of appropriate secluded and sheltered lakes. The first trip involved forcing our way through a cedar swamp while swatting mosquitoes and other insects. At one point I turned back to check on John, only to discover Lawrence of Arabia. He had taken a *keffiyeh* scarf from his camera bag and was wearing it with a confidence and grace that would have made Lawrence proud. This gift, received during his travels, was apparently effective in holding the insects at bay.

Several days later we placed a luggage rack on the top of my Volkswagen Beetle and loaded on a canoe to explore a few more distant lakes. We were on a strict schedule, as John had a meeting later in the morning with Dr. Harold Van Broekhoven to discuss the Institute of Theological Studies. My father joined us for the outing, and we began by exploring one or two lakes, but with no success. I suggested that there was one additional lake that we could just fit into the available time, and despite John's concerns that it might be wise to return for his meeting, we headed off down an old logging road filled with ruts and rocks. The trick to driving down this type of road is keeping the car tires on the rocks so they cannot damage the undercarriage. As we slowly pitched our way along I could see that John was not amused with this new phase of the venture.

Suddenly one of the tires slipped off a large rock, there was an ominous crunch, and the car engine began to race. I reversed off the rock and crawled under the car to assess the damage. One of the engine mounts had broken, with the result that the engine tipped toward the rear of the car, stretching the throttle cable. The engine ran well, but when I depressed the clutch it raced at high speeds, and when I released the clutch I found that I could not drive at speeds below 35 m.p.h. By depressing and releasing the clutch I could drive the car, but we would rocket ahead and then coast while the engine roared in neutral.

The trip back to Cedar Campus was several miles on back roads and we flew along, bouncing over ruts, skidding around corners in a cloud of dust and sounding like some kind of backwoods stock car racer. Throughout these events John was silent. We pulled up to the cabin, covered with dust and with the canoe swaying precariously on the roof rack. I glanced at my watch and commented that we were two minutes early for the meeting. John never said a word.

There were numerous other birding outings, though perhaps none as colorful. These times of birding were John's recreation, though he came to them with the same focus and intensity as he brought to his ministry. Reports to John of my travels would normally end with a quizzing of what birds had been seen along the journey. There were times when John would say wistfully, "I wish I could have been there to instruct you." His knowledge of birds, habitat and behavior was extraordinary.

In January 2006 I joined John and several other friends and Langham colleagues for a trip to China, John's last international trip. One crisp morning we stood outside the train station in Nanjing awaiting our train. Before us was Xuanwu Lake with numerous ducks in the distance. Lacking binoculars, we all made feeble attempts to identify the birds. I asked John what he thought and was stunned when he responded that he no longer watched birds. The series of small strokes that he had experienced in recent years had resulted in his not being able to see the birds clearly, so he had stepped away from his avocation. To me this was heartbreaking.

Three years later, in the week of the 2009 London snowstorm, Chris Wright and I ventured out to visit John at his new home at the College of St. Barnabas. John's health had failed further since his visit to China, complicated by a fall in the summer of 2006 that had resulted in a broken hip. We arrived to find John, to our surprise, reading through an early manuscript of Roger Steer's biography of him.[2] The natural question to ask was what he thought of the work, and we were both pleased to hear a positive response. But then John indicated that there was one serious problem. We both held our breath: was it a significant historical error? Had there been a misunderstanding of John's theological position on some issue?

No, the problem had to do with the 1942 sighting by John of a pair of black redstarts that had most unusually nested in London. The facts around the location were all wrong. John then went into a five-minute lecture on the habitat and behavior of the black redstart. The detail of this event and the breadth of information about this species were overwhelming. Suddenly the clock turned back to our many times in the field together over the previous decades. His eyesight was failing, but not his memory.

Given the stature of John Stott and his significant accomplishments, focusing on birds seems a bit mundane. But it was here that I found my best opportunities to get to know John personally and in contexts quite apart from his public role. His influence on me extends to almost all areas. I don't think I could unravel the many ways he has touched my life and the debt I owe him. One continuing joy is the large and ever-growing network of friends with similar experiences who are all part of Uncle John's family.

At a recent board meeting I had a few minutes of private conversation with John during a break in the proceedings. He was tired and had to work hard to concentrate on what I was saying. Suddenly he looked up and said, "I think what you mean is . . ." in his classic precise use of language, never missing an opportunity to instruct. I put my arm around him and said, "Uncle John, you have not changed in fifty years."

With a twinkle in his eye he replied, "Yes, it is a good thing, isn't it?"

Yes it is, a very good thing.

Salt and Light in the World of the Arts and Media

Nigel Goodwin

Nigel Goodwin, a graduate of the Royal Academy of Dramatic Arts, is the founder and executive director of Genesis Arts Trust, a ministry committed to serving the needs of Christian artists throughout the world, while also reaching out to those engaged professionally in the media/arts and entertainment industry. Nigel and his wife, Gillian, are mission partners of All Souls Church, originally invited by John Stott, who had taken an interest in their work and calling. They live on the Isle of Wight.

I am one privileged to serve as a missionary to the arts and media community worldwide. Having been called by God, the great Artist, in the 1960s, I was commissioned to this ministry by All Souls Church, as I sought to meet with, encourage and challenge gifted men and women working in the public arena of the arts. My constant aim was and is to help them think Christianly about the Author of their gift, and how their creative imagination could best serve the marketplace where they operate.

My wife, Gillian, and I began attending All Souls a few years after we were married in 1971. John Stott was by then Rector Emeritus, and Michael Baughen was rector. It was Michael who first invited us to become missionaries, and the church family has been a blessing to us ever since. John was still regularly preaching at All Souls when not fulfilling his global mission of bringing the whole gospel to the whole world. I had first heard and met him soon after my conversion to Christ in the summer of 1962. I had become an associate evangelist for the Movement for World Evangelisation (MWE), which ran a family holiday week at Filey in Yorkshire during mid-September each year.

In Ephesians 4:1-13, the apostle Paul speaks of the Christian's call and gift. Whether from the All Souls pulpit or fulfilling his global mission of bringing the whole gospel to the whole world, John Stott's preaching gift authenticated his amazing ministry. This work of grace has touched, and continues through his books to touch, thousands of individuals and communities worldwide. His preaching gift and biblical exposition opened up for me the riches, depths and wisdom found in Christ. When I first became a Christian in the early 1960s, it seemed to me that preaching was a dying art. Only a handful of preachers stood out. Of these Dr. Martyn Lloyd-Jones, my late father-in-law, George Duncan, and John Stott, profoundly and personally influenced my Christian walk.

Having spent a good part of my life in the performance arts, and by then already having engaged in a ministry to artists, I was acutely aware of the difference between truth and falsehood. John delivered truth with deep genuine conviction, yet with a winsomeness that drew one to deeper listening and greater comprehension.

David Brooks, the *New York Times* columnist, wrote on November 30, 2004, about John, "Stott is so embracing it's always a bit of a shock—especially if you're a Jew like me." Brooks continued:

[His] is a voice that is friendly, courteous and natural. It is humble and self-critical, but also confident, joyful and optimistic. Stott's mission is to pierce through all the encrustations and share direct contact with Jesus. Stott says that the central message of the gospel is not the teachings of Jesus, but Jesus himself, the human/divine figure. He is always bringing people back to the concrete reality of Jesus' life and sacrifice.

Many of us who were discovering faith in the 1960s were confronted by a church that had long since abandoned the concept that the media or the arts might be a valid calling for Christians. Sadly, evangelical culture and biblical interpretation caused a withdrawal from, even a hostility toward, Christian involvement in the surrounding culture. Put simply, if you wanted to be an artist, then you could not be a Christian. If you wanted to be a Christian, you could not be involved with the arts. You can imagine the pain and confusion this dichotomy created for many. John Stott, however, did not make such a division. On the contrary, he saw the arts as any other profession. If that was your gift, your calling, then you should remain within the situation in which you were called (1 Corinthians 7:24), because it is there that you will be both salt and light. That was his hugely encouraging message to people like me. All Souls Church became a haven, a shelter, for many in the media and arts.

On at least one occasion John visited our home for the then Arts Center Group in Kensington, London. He came to lecture on the subject of theology and art. John always encouraged robust apologetics, and great discussion ensued that evening. Voices such as his were few, but they rang true for their adherents. The authenticity of what he said was based on Scripture and not on cultural or personal opinions, and it shaped our thinking. The British rock-and-roll singer Cliff (now Sir Cliff) Richard, who had been my best man, was among those who attended All Souls whenever possible, and was greatly helped and encouraged by John's biblical exegesis and preaching.

I vividly recall John masterfully exercising his passion, wisdom and diplomacy at the first Congress on World Evangelization in Lausanne. Evangelicals from around the world were invited to gather and consider how they might develop a strategy for closer engagement with the world and a more effective witness to the gospel. I was there to give a workshop on the arts—something that was previously unheard of in such circles. I recall how a number of younger African, Asian and Latin American participants at Lausanne shared their poetry and their thinking about art and faith. Much of their work spoke to me of the anger and frustration they felt toward their parents, who were also present and who were first-generation converts to Christianity. Missions previously held in their own countries had shaped their thinking, but in the eyes of these their children, while embracing their new faith, they had given up their cultural roots and were in danger of becoming clones of the West. Their children, on the other hand, believed that to follow Christ gave a new freedom and a new identity, while not denying the roots of their own culture.

You can perhaps imagine the minefield that this tension produced, with so many countries in attendance. Lausanne's desire was to find a voice of unity. John was the right person, in the right place, at the right time. Grace and truth, which of course were only completely embodied in one person (John 1:14), were demonstrated with considerable rectitude and integrity by John Stott. With his skills of compassion and diplomacy, the conference came to a place of agreement, embracing unity in diversity, and the Lausanne Movement began. The missional value of Christian involvement in the arts and media has been recognized within the Lausanne Movement and has given rise to some important reflection and publication.[1]

To be members of a church such as All Souls has been to know a family which cares, loves and supports its members. To know John Stott as a friend and mentor, one who has been there to call upon and be encouraged by, has been for my wife and me a friendship of lasting value and privilege.

Did John have a favorite text? Somehow I doubt that, because the whole counsel of God has been his text. But I believe that these words from the book of Isaiah 60:1-3 are how John has conducted his pilgrimage with Jesus around the world:

Arise, shine, for your light has come,
    and the glory of the LORD rises upon you.
See, darkness covers the earth
    and thick darkness is over the peoples,
but the LORD rises upon you
    and his glory appears over you.
Nations will come to your light,
    and kings to the brightness of your dawn. (NIV)

29

THE LONDON INSTITUTE—FOUNDED BY "THAT FUNNY MAN IN THE FLOPPY HAT"

ANDREW KIRK

Andrew Kirk has taught missiology in Argentina (where he was involved in the earliest years of the Latin American Theological Fraternity) and in Birmingham, United Kingdom. He helped John Stott in the founding of the London Institute for Contemporary Christianity and was its associate director under John Stott from 1982 until 1990. He is now retired but still engaged in some writing and teaching in the United Kingdom and abroad.

Sitting in church one Sunday evening in 1960, listening to the passionate unfolding of the Word of God, was my first conscious recollection of John Stott. I was studying at the University of London. Christian students at that time used to frequent two major preaching and worship "temples": Westminster Chapel and All Souls. Being an Anglican, it was natural for me to attend the latter, although I did listen to the "Doctor" (Martyn Lloyd-Jones) occasionally. That particular sermon at All Souls stands out in my memory. The text was from Ephesians 1:6—"to the praise of the glory of his grace." Here was a person, steeped in the text, whose sole aim was to convey to the listeners, with the greatest clarity he could muster, the meaning of the life and work of Jesus Christ. What excited me, in contrast to some of the hypercritical and arid study of theology that I was being taught, was his fearless and enthusiastic commitment to the truth of the biblical message. I came away with a renewed confidence that it was all right after all to believe what the text affirmed to be true.

One of John's greatest gifts to the Christian community world-wide has been his meticulous attention to a faithful rendering of the meaning of Scripture, both in its original sense and in its translation and embodiment in the contemporary human life. That is why he paid so much attention to seeking out the correct principles of interpretation. Aware of the destructive, skeptical approaches to the text on the one hand and those that were at fault by being oversimplistic on the other, he struggled always for an understanding that was intellectually rigorous, spiritually nourishing and clearly contemporary.

My next recollection of John was a number of years later at the Lausanne Congress on World Evangelization in 1974. There can be little doubt that he was the main architect of one of the most remarkable documents to have come out of the evangelical stable. The Lausanne Covenant marked a watershed in evangelical thinking and has stood the test of time. It still remains a basic working document for evangelical cooperation across the globe.

The Fifth Assembly of the World Council of Churches (WCC) was held in Nairobi, Kenya, at the end of 1975. I participated as a delegate of the Anglican Church of the Southern Cone of South America (I was serving in Argentina at the time). John was also invited as a participant-observer and asked to give an address in one of the plenary sessions. The topic was "An Evangelical Perspective on Christian Social Engagement." Unfortunately for John and the whole audience, he was the last speaker, at the end of a long session. Undoubtedly, the organizers were not fair in their allocation of time. Nevertheless, John was characteristically humble and bold in his address. He focused on the twin themes of repentance for the neglect of social responsibility by evangelicals in their understanding of mission and a challenge to the WCC for its neglect of evangelism in its own perception of mission.

John was characteristically courageous in accepting that invitation from the WCC. At that time, following the meetings in Uppsala (1968) and Bangkok (1973), the WCC was perceived as a body that advocated the most extreme forms of liberal theology. Evangelicals were extremely wary of having anything to do with it. John, therefore, ran the risk of soiling his reputation as a leading evangelical statesman by associating himself with it. He, on the other hand, typically saw it as an opportunity to bear witness before this assembly to a more complete understanding of the truth of the gospel, and he did so with bold humility.

In 1977, John visited Argentina, where I was then working, after a long tour of Latin America. He was running a series of workshops on preaching, with René Padilla as his translator. The conference was held near the city of Córdoba in the center of the country. It was memorable for me not only because of the incisive and clear exposition of basic principles in preaching, but also for two other intriguing episodes that took place during the meeting. The first illustrates the complexities and hazards of translation. John was in full flow, with René doing an excellent job of rendering his address into Spanish. Suddenly, John interjected an idiomatic expression, so distinctively English that it completely defies translation: "setting the Thames on fire." Big pause. Lots of laughter from those in the audience who understood English while René tried valiantly to explain the reason for the interruption. The second incident, as might be expected, is a bird story. During one of the breaks in proceedings, John and I went for a stroll down a nearby path. Soon we heard the sound of a bird in the distance. It was unusual. Could it

be some exotic feathered species that even John had never set eyes
on? We silently crept close. We came to a fence. The bird song
seemed to be coming from the other side. We peered over. There
indeed was the bird on the other side—in a cage!

In the previous year (1976), a group of Christian leaders in Argentina (among them René Padilla and Samuel Escobar) set up an
educational institute for the purpose of exploring the embodiment
of the gospel in public life. It was given the name Kairos Community. I had the privilege of being a founding member. John, quite
independently, had been contemplating creating a similar kind of
institution in England. At the meeting in Córdoba we talked about
this aspiration. When, two years later, it seemed right for me and
my family to return to the United Kingdom, after twelve years in
theological education in Argentina, John invited me to be part of
the planning process that would lead to the setting up of an institution dedicated to the education of laypeople. The vision was to
offer programs that would encourage and equip ordinary Christians to work through the significance of the gospel for their experience of everyday life, especially in relation to secular culture and
the workplace.

After many meetings and the appointment of one or two permanent members of staff, the London Institute for Contemporary
Christianity was ready to go. At the end of April 1982, it opened
its doors to a first cohort of students from Britain and overseas,
invited to participate in a ten-week course focused on the meaning of Christian mission in the modern world. While the Institute's permanent home of St. Peter's Church, Vere Street, made
available by All Souls Church, was being refurbished for its new
role, the Institute met in the very agreeable surroundings of St.
Paul's, Robert Adam Street.

Although the inspiration for the Institute was the result of the
combined vision of a number of people (those involved in the
planning stage included Oliver Barclay, Os Guinness and Brian

Griffiths), the main driving force behind its initiation and development was John Stott. He was its first director. One of the principal reasons for its effectiveness lay with John's immense circle of friends and acquaintances. He was able to pull together a group of people from across the world willing to support the vision. These included a number of mature Christians willing to give their time on a voluntary basis (with expenses only) to undertake such essential tasks as building and running a library and a bookshop, tutoring students, and staffing the reception desk. Again, the factor that pulled people together was John's international stature as a conference speaker, writer and advocate for evangelical belief. He was a leader whom people from very diverse backgrounds trusted implicitly.

From the beginning of the Institute's life, John became known as "Uncle John." I have no idea where the title originated from. However, the first person I remember using the term was Dhyanchand Carr from South India, someone who had been associated with John during his student days in London. Everyone who came to study at the Institute was happy to use it. It spoke of our great affection for John, the cuddly side of his nature! Again, I don't know when or where John adopted the practice of greeting people with a hug. Certainly not, I would imagine, in the "Bash" camps, where he first learned what it meant to be a Christian. Perhaps it was in Latin America. At the end of one of his trips, he is reputed to have told the congregation at All Souls that he had learned three things in Latin America: enjoying a siesta, not minding when meetings began and kissing all the females in a room on entering. "However," he added, with a mischievous twinkle in his eye, "when I returned to England I had to unlearn two of the three, and I will leave you to guess which two!"

John had an excellent sense of humor. On one occasion, on a visit to our home for dinner, he presented a set of slides that he had taken on his 1977 journey around Latin America. Contrary to what might be expected, they were not all of birds, though the feathered friends did feature a few times! During this particular trip, he had been able to visit the Galapagos Islands off the coast of Ecuador (no doubt to see the famous finches). The islands are also renowned for their giant tortoises. Suddenly, there appeared on the screen a picture of John astride one of these magnificent animals. With amazement on her face, our small daughter piped up, "Who is that funny man with the large floppy hat?" Certainly, it was not John at his most elegant. Nevertheless, it was characteristic of the man to include it in the presentation.

The years at the London Institute were formative for me in many ways. I was grateful for the opportunity to work alongside John and see him engaging with so many different people in his own inimitable style. When talking to anyone, he was completely dedicated to that one person. His memory for names is legendary; so also is his recollection of the details of people's lives and backgrounds. Because of his international reputation, people might easily have felt intimidated in his presence. However, I do not think that this was the case for anyone, even the least significant. John was relaxed and immediately put people at their ease. He really cared about them and was humble enough to know that his own life would be enriched by getting to know them better. All of us were privileged to know him as a brother in the Lord and a faithful friend.

WELCOMING A REVOLUTION IN MUSIC

NOEL TREDINNICK

Noel Tredinnick has been director of music at All Souls Church since 1972. In addition, he pioneered the use of orchestral instruments in worship, the founding of the All Souls Orchestra, Langham Arts and the annual Prom Praise concerts at the Royal Albert Hall. He is also professor of conducting at the Guildhall School of Music and Drama.

It was 1972, the month was July, and it was a Sunday morning at All Souls, Langham Place. Although we had exchanged an initial brief and courteous greeting together in the vestry before the morning service, it was the bright, royal-red cassock that John Stott was wearing in his stall when leading the service that first impressed me and made an impact. I was the newly appointed organist and director of music, and this was my second Sunday taking up my fresh duties, and there, his back toward me, right beside our old downstairs organ console, stood this legend of a man, intoning in a somewhat unmelodic and single-toned voice the opening liturgy of the Anglican Morning Service.

In 1972 we still followed the full Anglican liturgy, although in those days we used a little white book with an updated English

version of the words of the confessions and other prayers. But it
was the brilliantly scarlet cassock that filled the chancel with personal color and certainly made a lasting impression on this new
recruit to the staff.

At that time, even though Michael Baughen had taken over
the newly created post of vicar of All Souls eighteen months earlier, we all used to wear our robes for services, and we followed
to the letter a contemporary liturgy. We also read from the Re-
vised Standard Version of the Bible, with copies available in
every pew seat. But it was in the music particularly that Michael
Baughen was already making his mark, by trying out new, updated versions of the Psalms—prototypes of congregational versions that would soon be collected into *Psalm Praise*. At my audi-
tion and interview, I'd been asked a lot about my views on the
use and development of contemporary Christian songs (as then
existed in the *Youth Praise* books), and I had been required to
demonstrate how I would play these on the organ—no chore for
me but a real, creative opportunity.

John Stott, I remember, really welcomed the lively, upbeat music
of these new, rhythmic congregational songs. He would beam as
he himself grappled with some new Baughen melody and text, and
he always persevered and congratulated us on these inspiring new
songs. He was nothing but hugely supportive of these growing
trends and experiments in contemporary hymnody and psalm-
ody—often commenting, always positively, and showing insight-
ful interest and involvement.

The same was certainly true when, for the Advent Sunday evening service in 1972, we first paraded our fresh, new All Souls
Orchestra. That was our inaugural appearance—maybe a bit un-
certain at first, but very soon gaining in effectiveness. John Stott
was an important part of our growing in stature and confidence,
with his continual interest and praise, his wise and helpful comments and occasional suggestions. That first night, as well as ac-

companying the hymn singing, the choir and orchestra presented Bach's cantata "Sleepers Awake!" as part of the evening service. John Stott could not contain his delight and congratulations. The orchestra appeared a couple of weeks later for carol services and then, after that, once a month when All Souls regularly held a guest service. From that time on, evangelism and orchestral music became inextricably linked at All Souls on Sunday nights on a monthly basis.

As a mark of his enthusiasm for (and dare I say his pride in) the emergence of the All Souls Orchestra (ASO), John Stott invited the players to lead the music at the National Evangelical Anglican Conference (NEAC) in 1977, held on the campus of Nottingham University beside the River Trent. The ASO conducted music workshops as well as leading all the robust singing in the large games hall, a powerful and memorable experience. Indeed, it was really a foretaste of what was to emerge in the Prom Praise concerts that started a year later. This NEAC exposure, together with regular appearances on BBC Television's *Songs of Praise* programs, helped establish around the world the reputation and influence of what was happening musically at All Souls.

John Stott so clearly loved the atmosphere of heartfelt singing and the rich tone that the orchestral playing engendered. This was often the subject of some comment and appreciation on both Monday and Wednesday lunchtimes, when staff members would gather in the rectory basement dining room and enjoy a cooked lunch together, with John at the head of the table when he was in residence.

John's cousin, Tamara Coates, a professional oboist and enthusiastic member of All Souls, was often involved, both in promoting and encouraging our music making. Like John, Tamara has bright-glowing cheeks, and she would beam her support either as player or congregational member. On my arrival I found that John had already nurtured the faith and the involvement of a number of other professional musical performers on a personal basis—Frank Boggs, the American bass gospel singer, was a regular contributor to our services, whom John hugely welcomed. And on the classical front the famous British soprano Jennifer Vivian enjoyed John's personal friendship, and she too would sing solos in services to the delight and joy of all who heard her.

Then there was the American connection that affected the musical style in All Souls, which can be traced to John's frequent visits across the Atlantic Ocean, the people he met there and the influences he encouraged us to introduce in London. Because they knew John, we had visits from Don Hustad, members of the Billy Graham team, Ron Owens and George Hamilton IV. My immediate predecessor as All Souls' organist, Clark Bedford, had been recruited by John from Pittsburgh, Pennsylvania, and he established something of an American-style music program, which I inherited.

Again through John's connections and requests in the United States, Kathryn Lynch of New York City donated the large sum of money that enabled the All Souls organ to be restored and extended in 1976. Martha Ashe, who regularly had John as a guest in her home in Florida, took a particular liking to the range of our musical style and repertoire ("that zippy music of yours," she used to call it). So she financed a number of important visits I made to the United States to share ideas and give the Americans a taste of All Souls music on their own soil. Actually this activity has now resulted in the formation of "Langham Arts America," which continues to allow the ASO some benefits and influence across the United States.

When John Stott celebrated his eightieth birthday in April 2001, we marked the occasion with a great concert and celebration in All Souls. John himself had been a cellist at Rugby School—and had continued to show some fascination and sensitivity toward that beautiful instrument of the orchestra. So as part of that concert, to recognize this aspect of John's own background, Jane Jewel contributed, with the ASO, a memorable and moving performance of the first movement of Elgar's Cello Concerto. That piece, for me, was certainly the highlight memory of those celebrations.

So, over the years, All Souls' music department has certainly benefited from the Stott legacy in terms of finance, visits and connections with creative artists and generous donors. And, all the time, John himself, with his own persistent observation, comment and positive interest (actually I cannot recall ever once getting any criticism at all from his lips), hugely encouraged, endorsed and praised the music ministry we have been attempting. And he loved the loud and vibrant congregational singing within All Souls. I have seen for myself how strong words, rich harmonies and soaring melodies, offered genuinely and from our hearts, have so nourished and coaxed his own prayer and worship. "All Souls music has enlivened my soul no end," he once told me.

Over all the years that Prom Praise concerts have been taking place, from 1977 in All Souls and then from 1988 in the Royal Albert Hall, John has been one of our most loyal fans and supporters. He would regularly buy up a number of guest tickets and use them to invite (and maybe influence) a number of his friends and contacts. I treasure the various thank-you notes he never failed to handwrite afterward, with his kindly expressed views and observations—and always his congratulations.

I once contributed a short article in a booklet about the life of All Souls, saying that, as musical director, my chief contribution was as a catalyst to encourage others to be involved and share their musical gifts. When that little article was first published, John took me aside after lunch one day.

"Dear brother Noel," he said, "I've been reading what you've written about your leadership here at All Souls. Of course you must do all you can to mentor and nurture others. But I can tell you, never devalue or ignore your own personal skills and contribution—who you are and what you can achieve yourself under God's almighty hand. You personally, through your own playing, leading and conducting, should never be underestimated either—I am profoundly grateful to God for the music you yourself make, as well as what you encourage and coax from others."

That was a helpful reminder to me from the great man—and it is a perspective I do try to bear in mind, even now.

THE STUDY ASSISTANTS

31

THE SERMON ON THE CARPET

MARK LABBERTON

Mark Labberton was one of John Stott's early study assistants. He went on to be senior pastor at First Presbyterian Church, Berkeley, California. He has served on the board of John Stott Ministries in the United States, and is now the Lloyd John Ogilvie Chair for Preaching at Fuller Theological Seminary, Pasadena, California.

The most memorable sermon I heard John Stott preach was not delivered at All Souls or at a large gathering in Asia, Africa or Latin America, or at a church or theological institution. Without a pulpit, surrounded by mud and standing only on a small piece of carpet honorifically brought forth for him, John preached on this occasion to a handful of people in a dark, dilapidated courtyard, surrounded by small fire pits, blackened pots and a set of simple homes.

This spontaneous sermon occurred as the outcome of a favor asked for by an Anglican priest serving in Burma. "Would it be possible," the priest wrote, "for John Stott to pay a pastoral visit to my elderly mother the next time he is in Madras, India?" Since the man served so far away from his mother, he wondered if John might well not get to her before he could, since she might not have long to live. He added, doubtless for extra motivation, that his mother was poor, declining in health, and "her teeth are falling out one by one."

On his next visit to Madras, John indeed took the scant information he had, more like the designation of large neighborhood than a house address, and set off with two of us to find this elderly lady. After a couple of hours of searching, passing under and through various layers of shacks and structures, we arrived at the door to the woman's home. She eventually emerged from the shadows, frail, nearly toothless, but smiling with a tearful joy. She knelt at John's feet and kissed them, and then she and John spoke through our translator for a few minutes. She made the request for a word of blessing, and once John had agreed, the carpet was brought forth and John prayed and offered his brief sermon.

The text was John 3:16. The words were simple and clear. The tone was compassionate and dignified. The assurance was personal and tender. The man who typically preached in a spotlight to hundreds and thousands, across a wide range of tribes and tongues and nations, with intellectual rigor and verbal command, now preached amid shadows to one woman and a handful of neighbors.

As his study assistant, accompanying John on this trip to India and Bangladesh, I was privileged with this view of John, the highly visible preacher, and John, the nearly invisible pastor. What struck me then and now was John's consistency in each role and his faithfulness to Christ in both. John was simply trying to love his neighbor, the priest in Burma, by serving his mother, the widow in India. All John did on that occasion was to fulfill a simple request. But to do so required personal persistence. It meant stepping away from the crowd—the same person, serving the same Lord.

My first exposure to John had occurred when I was twenty-three at IVCF's Urbana Student Missions Convention. The most captivating part of that week for me was the question-and-answer session that John led. Hundreds of people, out of the thousands at Urbana, showed up for this informal Q&A time.

I was greatly struck by the humility and clarity of John's responses, by his knowledge of the Bible and by his self-effacing humor.

At one point, a theological student asked a very long and technical question using many multisyllabic theological terms. John asked the young man first to define each of the words he had used, and second to restate his question more simply. It was, frankly, awkward and insistent—maybe even a little embarrassing—for the seminarian. He did as John had asked, however, and then John proceeded to respond to the question simply and clearly. Although I had not yet met John in person, this exchange suggested what I later found to be true of him: a drive for clarity, a confidence in rationality, an expectation of competency. John embodied these, even as he encouraged them in others.

While his demanding capacity and competence were impressive, what moved and intrigued me much more was his character. Who is this man? Is he who he seems to be? How did he become that person? Standing several years later in that darkened courtyard in India, I thought back to that Q&A session at Urbana. The integrity of John's life and ministry was not only apparent on stage but offstage as well. The humble and earnest devotion he expressed in public was also evident in private. John has sought to live one life serving one Lord.

Although I was a young Christian and recent seminary graduate at the time I came to work as John's study assistant, it had already become clear to me that while God provides gifts for ministry, the greater effect comes through character, the fruit of God's Spirit. Charisma, winsomeness, popularity, charm and cleverness can matter—in fact, they can matter too much. What endures and bears peculiar witness to God comes from beyond mere capacity before a crowd. The greater testimony comes in an otherwise un-explained character. This is what drew people to Jesus. This is what is meant to be true of Jesus' disciples.

The sermon on the carpet was the most memorable of John's sermons to me because it was the sermon that was John's life. His spiritual gifts might have taken him to India, to offer a set of lec-tures, to speak about important things with important leaders. But it was his character that got him into that darkened courtyard. The sermon he offered mattered not because of his degrees or his achievements or his honors, but because he had tasted that the Lord was good and had good news to share with an elderly sister in Christ who was blessed by that encouragement. The circum-stances that distinguished John's life from this woman's life were vast. But what they held in common mattered more, and they both knew that.

Over the three decades that I knew John, I have undoubtedly put him through some of the scrutiny that mentors often have to endure. I have wrestled internally with places of agreement and disagreement, with choices made or not, with our differences in attitude or experience, culture or generation. I don't have the same confidence in human reason that John does. I don't share the same rigorous commitment to self-discipline. The spiritual glass through which I look is not as clear as the one through which John sees. All that now seems like mere difference without division. For what still draws me to John more than anything else is the aroma of John's life—a life centered and matured in the love of Jesus Christ that bears fruit to the glory of God. John was all the more impressive, not less, the deeper our relationship became.

What I feared most from my early exposure to the Christian faith was that it seemed to make life smaller rather than larger—less love, less joy, less creativity, less wonder, less engagement. I was exposed to some pastors who seemed to be the incarnational proof that this was so. But when I came to faith in Christ as a young college student, I discovered that Jesus saves us from smallness.

I remembered this in Madras. As John preached that day, I stood so far from where I had been born and raised. I was now working for a pastor whose vision of the gospel had a cosmic and global reach, and who showed me in character and action that to be a disciple of Jesus meant growing in wisdom and love, in humility and hope. The world John knew and served was not parochial. The personal gospel was not a private one, and the particularity of the gospel was for the sake of its universality.

John introduced me to the Majority World, not as an object but as a family. His heart had grown far beyond his upper-class home and his elite education. He carried daily a vivid sense of the vital faith and strength of brothers and sisters around the world. He prayed daily as one standing alongside a very large family, with its size and urgency making it all the more compelling. I have experienced with peoples from many places and cultures our common center in Jesus Christ, and the ways our hearts and minds grew toward our Lord because of our brother, John.

What John taught me in that sermon in Madras was what his life has taught me over the last thirty years. God so loved the world that the gift of God's Son reorders and enlarges our hearts and our lives. The one gospel of our Lord and Savior Jesus Christ both intensifies and enlarges our understanding of God, and of the worth of our diverse brothers and sisters in Christ, and of all our earthly neighbors. The God who loves us all takes us where God wants, in order that we might show and proclaim this love for the transformation of the world and for the sake of God's glory. It was clear to me that day as John stood on the carpet in courtyard: John was simply being himself, the new self that was and is being renewed in the likeness of Jesus.

32

ICE CREAM AND CHOCOLATE SAUCE

TOBY HOWARTH

*Toby Howarth was John Stott's study assistant from 1986
to 1988. He is currently inter-religious affairs secretary to the
archbishop of Canterbury.*

How do I remember Uncle John, more than twenty years after
working with him (and the "omnicompetent" Auntie Frances) as
study assistant? I thank God for many things, and have struggled
too with his legacy in my life, but three things keep coming back
that I realize are now foundational to my faith.

The first is the basic truth, hammered home time and time
again from Uncle John, that Christians have a calling to be "salt
and light." The phrase comes from one of the best-known passages
in the entire Bible. Yet my experience with some Christians, as
well as others from different religious traditions, reminds me that
the vision for a faith community, deeply engaged in society for the
good of society, cannot be taken for granted. And although of
course that particular gospel thread runs through many traditions, it was Uncle John who first introduced it to me and to the
church within which I was nurtured.

Then, second, there is the longing for truth as well as unity among evangelicals that I witnessed firsthand while working for Uncle John. It was around that time that the book *Essentials* was published as a conversation between John Stott and David Edwards. The process of writing the book was in itself a major intellectual and theological challenge. As John said after a meeting with David, in which David began by being highly complimentary, "First the butter, then the dagger!" The publication of the book led to John being shot at from both sides—the more liberal and the more conservative. Most wounding of all were the letters and comments, even from close friends, as it became clear that he had distanced himself from the dogmatic certainty of many evangelicals about eternal conscious torment in hell as the fate of the unrepentant. But Uncle John wouldn't walk away from his convictions.

And the third thing was what I saw of his prayer life. It wasn't as contemplative or mystical as I then wished it to be. It was very rational, structured and disciplined. But it was no less personal for that. And one of our times of prayer together began in an embarrassing way, but ended in forgiving grace.

He had asked me to help with a light evening meal to which he had invited some people from All Souls. As usual the menu consisted of kebabs from a little shop around the corner, followed by ice cream and chocolate sauce. John had a great fondness for chocolate. (During a visit to India we had an arrangement whereby I filled a medicine bottle with Smarties, the British equivalent of M&Ms. After dinner on that visit, I would tell John that it was time for his Vitamin Ch and produce the medicine bottle.)

"Have you remembered to buy the ice cream?" John asked on the afternoon before the guests were due. "Yes, Uncle John," I replied, busy with something else and making a mental note to do it later. The trouble was, I didn't remember later, and by the time we had finished our kebabs, the shops were closed. There was no ice cream on which to pour the chocolate sauce.

The following morning I walked slowly up the stairs to his study to apologize. However, for Uncle John, it wasn't just a matter of saying "sorry." We talked through what had happened, and how our behavior as Christians relates to the character of God. Then we knelt on the floor of his study and prayed together.

He never mentioned the incident again.

33

"Above All, Cling to the Cross"

Corey Widmer

Corey Widmer was John Stott's study assistant from 1999 to 2002. Since 2005, he has been associate pastor of Outreach at Third Presbyterian Church, Richmond, Virginia, and since 2008, copastor of East End Fellowship, a multiethnic fellowship.

I have countless memories of my three years serving as Uncle John's study assistant, but two anecdotes are the most prominent in my mind. The first occurred after just a few months in the very mundane pattern of our daily life together. Every morning, at 11 a.m. sharp, I would bring him a cup of coffee. I would find him hunched over some letter or manuscript at his desk, consumed with the work before him, putting his unparalleled powers of concentration to whatever task was at hand. Not wanting to disturb him, I would quietly set the cup and saucer adjacent to his right hand, and oftentimes, he would mumble a barely audible word of thanks: "I'm not worthy."

Initially I thought this comment was amusing, but after a few months I began to find it slightly bothersome. How could someone pronounce himself unworthy of an acidic cup of instant coffee? One morning I was feeling a little cheeky, and when Uncle John mumbled his usual expression, "I'm not worthy," I quipped back, "Oh, sure you are."

Uncle John stopped, and I saw the powerful magnetic look of his concentration ease from the papers before him. He slowly raised his gaze, and, with a look of immense seriousness, yet boyish playfulness, he responded, "You haven't got your theology of grace right." I laughed, grinned awkwardly, and then said, "It's only a cup of coffee, Uncle John." As I turned round and headed back into the kitchen, I heard him mutter, "It's just the thin end of the wedge."

It took me days to figure out what he meant by that final rejoinder in our exchange. Though I never discussed it with him, I am convinced that he meant this: if our commitment to Jesus Christ and our understanding of his grace do not impact on the small places in our daily lives—the "thin end of the wedge"—then we are not living integrated lives. Our commitment to Christ may be most richly expressed in the most apparently inconsequential moments.

Uncle John was always fond of talking about "whole-life discipleship"—that is, his concern that the comprehensive lordship of Jesus Christ would extend its reign over every dimension of the Christian's life, bridging the "sacred-secular" divide that often separates our "spiritual" lives from our "secular" commitments and interactions.

I saw this same commitment deeply manifested in his daily life, in the way he carefully negotiated a simple lifestyle, in his concern for the physical and material environment, in his interactions with taxi drivers, waiters, hotel concierges and other sundry people who crossed his path, and above all in his gentle and winsome engagement with Frances and me on a daily basis. He truly was an "integrated" Christian, and the grace of the gospel infused even the thinnest ends of the wedge that was his life.

The second anecdote relates to a very different setting: in hot, balmy Madras, India. We were there for a preaching conference in 2002, and one afternoon while birdwatching, Uncle John took a nasty fall over a cement curb and lacerated his right leg. What looked to be a fairly harmless cut (one that would have healed naturally for someone less elderly) soon became a painful, swollen and infected wound, and began to worsen daily. Over two days we visited at least three different doctors in several different hospitals, but no treatment seemed to be halting the wound's deterioration. Finally, I was able to get in touch with Uncle John's cardiologist back in London, and with grave concern in his voice the doctor warned me of the immense seriousness of the situation in view of the state of Uncle John's heart. He insisted that if things did not improve immediately, we should come back to London as soon as possible.

Later that day Uncle John and I were together in his room as I recounted to him the concern of his doctor. It was as solemn a moment as I ever shared with him. I believe that both of us perceived that, with the real possibility of serious infection and blood poisoning, these could possibly be his last days on the earth. Despite this fact and the pain that he was experiencing, he remained lighthearted and engaging, as always. Almost as if he recognized that this might well be some of the last time we would share together, he began talking with me about my future, about my desire to be a pastor, about what he considered the most vital dimensions of the pastoral ministry. Of all that he shared with me in those precious moments, one piece of advice has stayed with me more than any other: "Above all," he said, "cling to the cross."

The cross of Christ, the title of what he considered his most important book and the one in which he invested more of himself than any other, was the paramount theme, the one he returned to again and again. He took quite literally Paul's call in Galatians 6:14, one of his "life verses" as he often called it, to be "obsessed" with the cross. Even when he was not speaking about it directly, the centrality of the cross remained like a deep subterranean undercurrent beneath the body of Uncle John's life and work, affecting and directing so much of his thinking on ethical, theological and pastoral issues. "The Pervasive Influence of the Cross" is the title of the epilogue of *The Cross of Christ*. It could just as well serve as an epilogue for his life.

Thankfully, Uncle John's leg did heal, and several more years of ministry lay ahead for him beyond that moment in India. Those were not his final words to me, as it turned out. But for me, they endure beyond all others.

34

"WATCH OUT! I USED TO BE A BOXER!"

MATTHEW SMITH

Matthew Smith was John Stott's study assistant from 2002 to 2005. After working for two years as an economist in Sierra Leone, he is now involved in public sector reform projects in developing countries.

Uncle John often joked, when introducing me to friends, that he'd known me since before I was born! It was a valid claim in that he was certainly instrumental in my father's conversion and early Christian life, and he had officiated at my parents' wedding. One story I remember through the mists of time was when Uncle John and Michael Wilcock came to visit our home in Bristol when I was three or four years old. The conversation, which probably revolved around friends and theology, must have been a bit too much for me, as I somewhat impolitely inquired at the dinner table, "Daddy, when are they leaving?" Uncle John's reply diffused the embarrassment: "Poor Matthew isn't receiving the close attention he's used to!"

Skip forward twenty-two years to another occasion when Uncle John, along with his then study assistant Corey Widmer and his wife, Sarah, came to stay with my parents. Uncle John inquired about how my career in accountancy was progressing and what my next steps were, but since it was so characteristic of him to be interested in the details of people's lives, I didn't pick up on the detective work that was going on. After waving goodbye to Uncle John at the end of the weekend, I remember saying to my family how I would love to become Corey's successor! So it was with huge excitement that I received a letter later that week from Uncle John, inviting me to be his next study assistant. What followed was an inspiring three years, working with a boss who was already a lifelong mentor and now became a close friend.

When we first discussed the idea of this *Portrait*, back in 2005, with Frances Whitehead and Chris Wright, Uncle John in his humble way was keen for a frank and honest picture to be painted. For example, he asked me to mention the self-pity he sometimes fell into when work got on top of him! Certainly, in his later years, Uncle John has struggled with increasing age and decreasing physical and mental capacities, but he has done so with incredible grace. In one conversation, when he was talking about the humiliating loss of faculties through age, he also reflected on the secret treasures of the changing relationships that such increasing frailty brings.

Uncle John was able to push back the years and continue writing into his late eighties, partly through his incredible drive and discipline, but also through a strong sense of duty and conviction. I witnessed his great powers of perseverance throughout my time as his study assistant, but perhaps most particularly during the writing of *Through the Bible Through the Year*.[1] It was obviously a huge task, seeking to comment selectively on the whole Bible. The early stages of the project were particularly difficult, with most of the book still to write and when he was covering Old Testament topics, where he felt less at ease. Uncle John sometimes became discouraged with lack of progress, but he simply battled through! Indeed he thrived on work. Once, when convalescing from a fall and a nasty cut that he had sustained at the reopening of The Hookses in September 2004, he commented, "I think if I see paper in front of me I will immediately improve!"

In terms of routine, we generally spent about six months of the year in and around London, three months at The Hookses, and three months traveling internationally. Uncle John's term for our small team of three (himself, Frances Whitehead and the study assistant) was "the happy triumvirate." One of my favorite occasions during our time in London was the happy triumvirate's team breakfast, which was hosted by Uncle John in his flat and began each Monday at 8 a.m., though Frances would generally arrive a few minutes early so that she could first catch up with the weekend's events. I'd knock at the bottom of the winding stairs to Uncle John's study/living room and would be warmly welcomed by a ringing "Come in, come in" and a small glass of orange juice. We'd have muesli together and then (except in Lent when Uncle John would refrain) enjoy a slice of toast, butter and often Frances's homemade marmalade. After breakfast we would open our diaries and plan for the week ahead, and then get down on our knees for a time of prayer.

Uncle John was indeed a meticulous planner, and this was sometimes taken to extremes—for example, much to my amusement, shopping trips (which were rare enough events) would be scheduled two or three weeks in advance! Such trips were, however, worth waiting for and great fun. No sooner had we entered a shop than Uncle John seemed to want to leave! He'd stride in with purpose and then probably purchase the first of whatever particular product he would see—browsing was certainly not one of his enjoyments.

One particular experience on Oxford Street, not to be forgotten, was when we were going to the cinema with the then All Souls youth worker Adam Rushton. Uncle John liked the cinema and also enjoyed meeting new members of the All Souls staff team.

We walked down from Weymouth Street, and as we approached Oxford Street I foolishly mentioned that the bus ahead of us was the one we needed to catch, so we both broke into a jog. Now, because of John's weakening eyesight, I had been trained by Corey always to look ahead of Uncle John's footsteps, but on this occasion I was looking at the bus and didn't see a large crack in the pavement. Nor, unfortunately, did Uncle John. He literally flew through the air, landing quite heavily on his left knee and grazing his hand. Fortunately the wounds were superficial, and there was a pharmacy close by, so we were able to get him patched up before going on to the film. When I apologized for my part in the accident, Uncle John uttered one of his favorite cures for those with overscrupulous consciences: "FG," he said, "false guilt!"

The journey to The Hookses was something we both looked forward to immensely. I had it a bit easier than my predecessors, since I was granted a later 6:30 a.m. start. After our opening prayer for the journey and questions about the time I had gone to bed the previous night, we'd set off on the road out of London. And immediately we'd begin our mobile Bible study, which was usually based on what Uncle John or I was reading at the time. He would read the passage and open the reflections, and then we'd exchange ideas about the particular challenge or encouragement that it brought, while I continued to drive in the inside lane—my concentration being split between carrying precious cargo and trying in vain to add anything to what Uncle John had already said! Next we'd have our sung rendition of "Awake My Soul," in all its beautiful eight verses. Then I'd be treated to a large fried breakfast at a motorway service station along the route. After that would come the talking book: Agatha Christie, Sherlock Holmes or P. G. Wodehouse were the favorites.

The Hookses' routine changed during my time as study assistant in that Uncle John's afternoon hour of exercise became understandably less energetic. In 2002 we would still push a wheelbarrow up to the airfield and shovel sods of turf from the edge of the runway back down into the garden area. By 2005 we would perhaps just go for a brief walk round the coastal footpath, or Uncle John would supervise me doing the strimming of the grass, or we would tackle some DIY jobs in the house. The Hookses was the ideal place to concentrate on research activities. We also became involved in the life of the village and I learned there the importance of visiting people.

It always staggered me how Uncle John was able to maintain meaningful relationships with so many people around the world. He was great at building bridges with those of all ages, classes and races, and this was helped by his exceptional ability to remember names and personal details—no doubt aided by his regular prayer for his friends. He was a very careful listener, and often in conversation he would be more keen to ask questions than to express his own views. He also maintained a fantastic repertoire of stories and anecdotes, and was extremely quick-witted. He asked me once if I was going to have the day off, since it was a Bank Holiday (the term for public holidays in the United Kingdom). I said yes, and then asked him if he was going to do the same. "No, no, no," he replied. "Why not?" I asked. "Because I'm not a bank!" he retorted with glee. He had a great sense of fun, and I will never forget the sparkle in his blue eyes after some quip or other, or the occasional moment when he would literally cry with laughter over some amusing story.

Uncle John didn't suffer fools gladly and could be direct when he needed to be. He also knew how to defend himself. One day while walking home in London, then in his early eighties, he was subjected to an attempted mugging. A man came up behind him, put his hands over his eyes and demanded his wallet. Uncle John gave him a sharp dig in the ribs, said he would not give him his wallet, and exclaimed, "Watch out! I used to be a boxer!" The man ran off, and Uncle John strode on up to Weymouth Street! (He had indeed boxed as a boy at school.)

He couldn't easily tolerate any form of hero worship or flattery—in fact he became visibly embarrassed every time he was given an overly long or exaggerated introduction to the speaker's platform. The inclusion of John Stott as one of *Time* magazine's "World's Most Influential People" in 2005 was genuinely surprising to him. As he said to Frances and me once, "I don't like mingling with the mighty! I'm just an ordinary bloke, and these favors don't fit comfortably on my shoulders."

Uncle John lived a simple lifestyle. When traveling, he always preferred to stay in someone's home rather than in an expensive hotel, and he would insist on traveling economy class for even the longest of trips. It was only with the increasing threat of deep-vein thrombosis that he allowed his travel agent to book premium economy on transatlantic trips. Nevertheless I always tried to get him upgraded to a better seat, if possible in business class. But then he would often tease me for giving the female check-in assistants, as he said, the "glad eye"! Despite being deliberately careful with spending on himself, I often observed his generosity to others. In this, as in so many areas, he genuinely practiced what he preached.

A personal portrait of Uncle John cannot be complete without mentioning Frances Whitehead. Working with Frances was a huge privilege, and her industriousness, inquisitiveness and overall wisdom and guidance were invaluable. She knew Uncle John's mind better than anyone. Uncle John used to joke that his study assistant was sometimes right, he was mostly right and Frances was always right! Such was the hierarchy of correct decision making in the happy triumvirate. Frances was known as a fierce protector of Uncle John's diary, an unenviable position in which she was placed by his tendency to fill it beyond capacity. For Uncle John didn't like declining invitations—he saw these as part of his overall ministry. Frances's role in Uncle John's life and ministry was indispensable. As he said to me once, "I do hope that I predecease Frances. I don't think I'd be able to live without her!"

Uncle John has no doubt mellowed with age. I didn't work with him in the years when he would write a chapter each day, drive fast along country lanes and arrive just in time at airports. I got to know him in his eighties, when his pace of life and relative productivity were declining. However, even then, like my predecessors, I had to run to keep up with him. I am so grateful that I was study assistant at a point in his life when Uncle John could give me time to spend with him—lunchtimes in his flat with our turkey and ham sandwiches, going for a walk round the Rose Garden in Regent's Park, which he remembered from boyhood, receiving wise advice on so many occasions, being taught to distinguish bird songs in the Pembrokeshire countryside, having dinner in the drafty and prerenovation The Hookses dining room.

I cannot adequately capture in this short piece the things I have learned from Uncle John or the fun and fellowship I have enjoyed with him, but suffice to say I know he was truly exceptional in character, achievement and godliness.

THE FINAL LAP

"I Have a Living Hope of a Yet More Glorious Life Beyond Death"

JOHN WYATT

John Wyatt is professor of ethics and perinatology at University College Hospital, London. He is also a member of the ethics committees of the Royal College of Physicians and the Royal College of Paediatrics and Child Health, and active in the Christian Medical Fellowship. He is well-known as a speaker and writer on issues of medical ethics. He and his wife, Celia, are members of All Souls Church.

I first met John when I was a lowly medical student, soon after I started attending All Souls in the 1970s. To my amazement and immense delight, he invited me to his flat for a cup of coffee. There followed a gentle but searching cross-examination about my family background, Christian journey, musical interests (I was a member of the newly formed All Souls Orchestra) and my proposed medical career. But I remember right from the start of our friendship his remarkable openness, honesty and humility, and the courtesy and respect with which he treated me and all the ju-

nior members of the church family. As many others have commented, John has a remarkable gift for establishing and maintain-
ing friendships.

There have been particular moments in my own life, times of
celebration and times of deep darkness, when his friendship has
meant a great deal to me. One moment in particular still brings
tears to my eyes, when I remember hearing his voice on the telephone. I was in deep despair and confusion, having been admitted to a locked hospital ward following an acute mental break-
down. "I value your friendship, John," he said to me. I was deeply
moved that he had taken the trouble to track me down and make
that call.

I have no doubt but that experience brought us closer together
when our roles were reversed some years later. John was admitted
to hospital for emergency surgery, following his fall in August
2006 when he broke his hip. It was a great privilege for me to
spend some time with him nearly every day during his hospital
stay. Immediately following the surgery, he had periods of confusion and visual hallucinations, which lasted for several days. This
caused him great concern, as he feared he was permanently losing
his mind, although at other times he was perfectly orientated and
compos mentis. I remember how we laughed and wept together
over the indignities and petty humiliations of hospital life, and the
alarming frailty of our bodies and our brains.

On returning from hospital to his beloved bachelor flat in Bridford Mews, he was occasionally emotionally overwhelmed by the
implications of his severely weakened physical condition and his
lost independence. He was somewhat taken aback by the force of
his emotions and struggled to understand himself. He had never
been prone to detailed self-analysis, and for most of his life he
tended to take his robust physical health and mental equanimity
for granted. But the novel experience of "blubbing," as he irrever-
ently called it, has been moving and liberating, and has brought a

new dimension of mutual vulnerability and openness to the relationship between us.

Later on when he asked my advice on a medical matter, I remember teasing him that as a babies' doctor I was completely useless to him; in fact the only useful knowledge I had was on diaper rash, to which he replied, "I hope it hasn't come to that yet, dear brother."

As the son of an eminent Harley Street (a London medical center) consultant, John inherited a traditional respect for the medical profession.

However, he was always acutely aware of the medical hierarchy. The diagnosis of the senior consultant was of unquestionable accuracy and his instructions were to be recorded, noted and followed *ipsissima verba;* the registrars and GPs were to be listened to but were quite capable of fallibility; the opinions of nurses and other health professionals were well-meaning but of little consequence.

With his failing health, we encouraged him to write a legally valid document providing a statement of his wishes and concerns, which could be used by his treating doctors if he became incapacitated or unconscious. This is what he wrote, characteristically bringing his Christian convictions to bear on the matter.

> I greatly value the ability to think clearly, to be able to write, to be physically independent and to be able to meet and provide pastoral support to friends and contacts. If I am suffering from a treatable condition in which it is likely that a relatively short period of medical treatment will restore me to my present health and mental functioning, then I would like to receive such treatment. However, I would not wish my life to be artificially prolonged if thereby I am left in a terminal or vegetative state. . . . The reason that I do not wish to cling to life is that I have a living hope of a yet more glorious life beyond death, and I do not wish to be

unnecessarily hindered from inheriting it.

A regular theme of his preaching and writing has been the reality of human frailty and of our utter dependence on God, the God who himself enters into the human experience of weakness and dependence. I remember him once talking about his habit, when walking alone, of remembering that every fresh breath, every heartbeat, was a gift from God which could be taken away at any time.

But the practical reality of increasing physical dependence and memory loss was not at all easy for him to bear. As someone with a lifelong razor-sharp intellect, he found the memory lapses and occasional confusions of old age painful and at times humiliating, although he rarely admitted how much he felt the loss. He continued to preach at All Souls, and at times his sermons had us on the edge of our seats as he suddenly lost track of his thoughts and we wondered whether he would recover. With his usual self-deprecating sense of humor, he frequently made fun of his own "decrepitude."

Characteristically, he remained his own severest critic. During the period after his fall, while struggling to come to terms with the implications, I remember him saying to me that he was deeply disappointed that "after so many years of living as a Christian I am still capable of such self-preoccupation and selfishness."

He had always defined himself in terms of Christian service, and the realization that his public ministry was coming to an end was particularly painful for him. But he accepted his losses with Christian fortitude, with patience and with good humor. "Like Paul, I am learning the secret of being content in every situation. I would not say that I am happy but I am content."

Above all, John's desire was to "finish well"—to continue to incarnate the life-changing Christian truth he had preached and taught, to humbly worship the Lord he has served, in "living hope of a yet more glorious life beyond death."

Epilogue

CHRIS WRIGHT

I begin this epilogue on the train back to London after visiting John Stott, along with Jonathan and Margaret Lamb. And I begin with a note of thankfulness for the staff at the College of St. Barnabas, Lingfield, the Christian care community where John has lived since 2007. Their loving attention to his special needs in these years of increasing debility has been a great comfort and relief to all of us who hold him dear. He was pleased to hear that this *Portrait* by his friends has been completed, even though several of those who have contributed to it have gone ahead of John into the presence of their Lord before its publication.

Reading again through all the preceding chapters, one can anticipate a question that is bound to arise in the minds of readers who did not know John personally: "Isn't this all just too good to be true? Is the portrait not too perfect? Had the man no faults and failings?"

John himself, of course, would be the first to say that he knew his own failings only too well. In the later years of his increasing frailty, after his fall and broken hip in 2006, he found it hard to cope with the relentless frustration of reduced capacity after a lifetime of extraordinarily productive activity. He confessed that he was amazed at how illness, pain and lack of mobility could reduce him to self-pity and self-centered words and actions. And that from a man whose whole life had been selflessly given to his Lord and to others, with countless tokens of generosity and thoughtfulness as recorded in these pages. But he was human and knew his faults. However, he knew the precious grace of divine forgiveness even more, and the two combined in that deep and utterly genuine humility that so characterized him. I once shared with him a consciousness of specific sin and failure in my own life, as I felt the need to "walk in the light" as we started working together. With gentle grace and no hint of reproach, he simply murmured, "Welcome to the wonderful fellowship of the forgiven."

There is a great British institution known as "a stick of rock." It's a stiff, sweet candy produced at seaside resorts, cylindrical and usually about 12 inches long, so that it can endure a week or more of sucking and chewing. Every stick of rock will have lettering running through the inside, either some "good luck" slogan or the name of the seaside resort. So the saying goes: "Wherever you break a stick of rock, the words are the same all the way through." It's an image that comes to mind when I think of John Stott. Not only was he a rock of a man in that other sense—a strong fortress of evangelical conviction, a robust but gracious defender of the faith, a rock of strength, prayer and encouragement to hundreds of friends around the world. But like a seaside stick of rock, he was the same all the way through. It seemed that wherever you might break him open, the lettering would be the same: the message of his life and his words was consistent. What words might you have found in that lettering? Some spring to mind at once: humility, integrity, simplicity, self-discipline, diligence, grace . . .

And that raises another question: what should be the impact of a life like that? Inspiring certainly. But to be emulated? More than one of his study assistants, who got to know him at close quarters probably better than most, have said to me that they started out hoping to live like "Uncle John"—to match up to his daily habits of self-discipline, prayer and hard work. But in the end they could not, and though they could admire and aspire, the attempt to imitate was a recipe for alternating pride or frustration—not to mention the dangers of hypocrisy. One, who would doubtless prefer to remain nameless, said that when he was with John at The Hookses, he would set his alarm for 5 a.m. and switch his light on, knowing that John would be rising at that time for his prayers—and then he (the study assistant) would go back to sleep, leaving the light in his window sending its misleadingly pious signal.

And yet, I wonder. We may think of John as undoubtedly exceptional, but he was not superhuman. His life was one of utterly committed self-discipline in what he believed to be the way a disciple of Jesus should live. And is that not in principle what all of us are called to? When I find myself saying, "I simply could not be like John in personal devotion and detailed regular prayer for so many friends," my heart answers, "Why not?" It is not that I could not but that I do not. So at the very least the exemplary life of John Stott is a challenge, a question, a rebuke, an encouragement, an inspiration, all in one. And one has to add, of course, that for all the regime and routine he imposed on himself (and others), for all his iron self-discipline, he never lost the softer graces of just being human—his love for children, his easy relating to families, his great sense of humor and laughter, his appreciation of cultures, his passion for birds and the rest of creation, his compassion for the poor and needy, the huge warmth of his hugs, his childlike love of chocolate . . . And in those dimensions too (except perhaps the chocolate), he reminds us above all of Jesus Christ. It is not surprising, then, that several contributors have spoken of John as "the most Christlike person they have known." Perhaps, then, the key thing (John would agree) is not to try to imitate him but to imitate the Christ who so demonstrably lived within him.

And that brings me back to the stick of rock. We may think of many words that run through the life of John Stott. But what lettering would John himself want us to find there if we broke the stick at any point? I think he would say either "A sinner saved by grace" or "A simple follower of Jesus." The first was what he knew himself to be, the second what he longed to be more than anything else. I have been with him on occasions when the praise and flattery were ecstatic, and have heard him quietly say, "People say such silly things," and I know he was mentally and spiritually deflecting the honor and glory to the Lord Jesus Christ.

And that is how I am certain he would want this *Portrait* to end, and what he would want its effect on its readers to be. He would remind us of his two favorite verses. The first was Galatians 6:14—in the King James Version in which he usually quoted it:

> God forbid that I should glory, save in the cross of our Lord Jesus Christ, by whom the world is crucified unto me, and I unto the world.

The second was John 14:21, 23, the powerful words of Jesus:

> Whoever has my commands and keeps them is the one who loves me. The one who loves me will be loved by my Father, and I too will love them and show myself to them. . . . Anyone who loves me will obey my teaching. My Father will love them, and we will come to them and make our home with them. (NIV)

From his conversion and through all his life, John Stott gloried in the cross of Christ and its atoning power, and preached the gospel of salvation by grace alone through faith. Like the apostle Paul, he longed to bring people to "the obedience of faith" at the foot of the cross. And there are thousands around the world who have been led to faith in Christ through the preaching and writings of John Stott.

But John was equally passionate about what might be called "the obedience of love"—that is, our obedience to the teachings of Jesus, which alone can prove the reality of our claim to love him. So much of his own preaching and writing was about the down-to-earth practice of radical Christian discipleship in the home, the workplace—everywhere in fact. "It's no use," he would say "just singing pretty songs: 'Jesus, I love you.' They don't prove anything. It's only in daily life that you prove, through obedience, whether or not you love Jesus."

John Stott, then, was a man who spent his life leading people to trust in the cross of Christ and urging those who had done so to obey the words of Christ. So to the extent that this *Portrait* speaks the truth about the man it portrays, let it also portray the transforming truth of the gospel of our Lord Jesus Christ in the life of one of his most dedicated followers. And for that life we give all the glory, thanks and praise to the Lord our God.

Chris Wright

Notes

Preface
[1]John Eddison, ed., *"Bash": A Study in Spiritual Power* (London: Marshall, Morgan & Scott, 1983).

Chapter 2: The Wedding Sermon
[1]The All Souls Clubhouse opened in 1958 as a community and Christian center in the eastern part of the All Souls parish.

Chapter 6: "It Takes Just Seven and a Half Minutes"
[1]The annual meeting for evangelical Anglicans of the Church in Wales; when it outgrew The Hookses it met in the local church at Dale.

Chapter 10: "I Have Got My Sins, You Have Got Yours"
[1]The Wednesday Club was started in the 1940s for young people from about seventeen to mid-twenties. It met on Wednesday evenings, hence the name!

Chapter 13: "Dragged Screaming into the Modern World"
[1]Darrell W. Johnson, *The Glory of Preaching: Participating in God's Transformation of the World* (Downers Grove, Ill.: InterVarsity Press, 2009), p. 7.
[2]David Wells, "Guardian of God's Word," *Christianity Today*, September 16, 1996, p. 56.
[3]Alister McGrath, in *J. I. Packer and the Evangelical Future*, ed. Timothy George (Grand Rapids: Baker Academic, 2009), p. 21.
[4]Mark Noll, *The Scandal of the Evangelical Mind* (Downers Grove, Ill.: InterVarsity Press, 1994), p. 253.

Chapter 15: The Prolific Author and His Midwife
[1]Timothy Dudley-Smith, *John Stott: A Comprehensive Bibliography* (Downers Grove, Ill.: InterVarsity Press, 1996).

[2]John Stott, *The Birds Our Teachers* (Worthing West Sussex, U.K.: Candle Books, 1999).

Chapter 16: A Double Portion of Language Skills

[1]John Stott, *The Message of the Sermon on the Mount* (Downers Grove, Ill.: InterVarsity Press, 1978).

Chapter 18: On the Road with John Stott

[1]*The Willowbank Report: Consultation on Gospel and Culture*, Lausanne Occasional Paper 2, 1978, www.lausanne.org/all-documents/lop-2.html.

[2]*Evangelism and Social Responsibility: An Evangelical Commitment*, Lausanne Occasional Paper 21, 1982, www.lausanne.org/all-documents/lop-21.html.

Chapter 24: The Boy with the Disappearing Eyes

[1]Saki, "The Storyteller," in *Beasts and Super-Beasts* (1914; reprint, Whitefish, Mont.: Kessinger, 2004).

Chapter 26: Birding Before Dawn Around the World

[1]*Feijoada* is a typical Portuguese stew of beans with beef and pork.

Chapter 27: The Call of the Loon

[1]A gadwall, a duck common across Europe, Asia and North America.

[2]Roger Steer, *Basic Christian: The Inside Story of John Stott* (Downers Grove, Ill.: InterVarsity Press, 2010).

Chapter 28: Salt and Light in the World of the Arts and Media

[1]For example, *Redeeming the Arts: The Restoration of the Arts to God's Creational Intention*, Lausanne Occasional Paper 46, www.lausanne.org/documents/2004forum/LOP46_IG17.pdf.

Chapter 34: "Watch Out! I Used to Be a Boxer!"

[1]John Stott, *Through the Bible Through the Year* (Grand Rapids: Baker, 2006).

JOHN STOTT MINISTRIES

John Stott Ministries is the U.S. chapter of the Langham Partnership International (LPI), a network of three integrated programs—Literature, Preaching and Scholars—which was founded by John Stott. Chris Wright serves as the International Ministries Director.

Langham Literature (formerly the Evangelical Literature Trust), a program of Langham Partnership International, is the sole recipient of all royalties from this book.

Langham Literature distributes evangelical books to pastors, theological students and seminary libraries in the Majority World, and fosters the writing and publishing of Christian literature in many regional languages. Langham Preaching establishes movements for biblical preaching in many countries, training people in how to study and preach the Bible in their own contexts, with continuous learning in local preachers' networks. Langham Scholars provides funding for gifted leaders to study for doctorates in the Bible and Theology, and return to their home countries to teach future pastors in seminaries.

For more information, please visit the
John Stott Ministries website at <www.johnstott.org>
and the LPI website at <www.langhampartnership.org>.